Meditations for Survivors of Suicide

JONI WOELFEL

Resurrection Press
An Imprint of
CATHOLIC BOOK PUBLISHING CORP.
Totowa • New Jersey

First published in September, 2002 by

Catholic Book Publishing/Resurrection Press

77 West End Road

Totowa, NJ 07512

Copyright © 2002 by Joni Woelfel

ISBN 1-878718-75-4

Library of Congress Catalog Card Number: 2002107687

The scripture quotations contained herein are from the New Revised Standard Version Bible: Catholic edition, © 1989, by the Division of Christian Education of the National Council of the Churches of Christ in the U.S.A. Used by permission. All rights reserved.

Cover art by Mary Southard, CSJ, © 1997 Sisters of St. Joseph of LaGrange

Design by Beth DeNapoli

Printed in the United States

2 3 4 5 6 7 8 9

We know that every moment
is a moment of grace,
Every hour an offering;
Not to share them
would be to betray them.

Our lives no longer belong to us alone;
They belong to all
who need us so desperately.

—*Eli Wiesel*

I dedicate this book to my beloved family:
My husband Jerry
My son Damian and partner Rachel
My son Dana and daughter-in-law Jennifer

In Loving Memory of our Dominic (Mic)
Forever missed, always in our hearts
October 30, 1981 - August 7, 1999

Contents

Acknowledgments

THE writing of this book is one of the most significant things that I will ever accomplish in my lifetime. As it began unfolding, my goal was not for it to be a 'perfect' book, but rather a book that sought wholeheartedness of spirit. It is only through the influence of others that this became possible. My deepest gratitude goes to Adolfo Quezada, Sister Ave Clark, O.P., Antoinette Bosco, Judy Osgood and Lillian Meyers for taking me under their wings when Mic died and teaching me that I could survive. Through their voices of courage and the visionary perspective of faith that they live, I began to see that I, too, could find the way. There are no words to express how honored I feel to call them friends and colleagues.

To Greg Pierce, my publisher at ACTA, I extend my greatest appreciation for the life-changing opportunities he afforded me, always believing in both me and my work and extending the hand of friendship. I also thank my editor, Rich Heffern from the *National Catholic Reporter* for his compassion and support as well as Arlene Goetz, my editor at Catholic Women's Network. Julie Buntjer, my editor at the *Wabasso Standard,* I thank especially for her kinship and earnest belief in the importance of being proactive. Also, I would like to thank Ann Ruethling and Janet Kelly from Isabella for all their care.

Many people have prayed for our family and this book. I extend my deepest appreciation to all, especially to Frances Placentra, my daughter-in-law, Jennifer Woelfel, and Rachel Abernathy. I must also thank my trio of soul-friend consultants, Libbie Adams, Ann Poplawski and the late Sharon Allard. Special thanks are extended to Terry Krier, who offered validation and affirmation of this work in the memory of his beloved son, Mathias. To Jeb King, I send thanks for his realism and unique ability to inspire me to look on the light side in many aspects, both deep and humorous.

As the web master of our web site, Gary Frye has provided invaluable dimensions to this ministry. I can never thank him enough. Jerry and I also extend special thanks to Dee Frye for her beautiful sweatshirt, T-shirt and business card designs. Accolades to them both as well as warmest thanks to our close community of friends at the web site message boards.

Finally, there are no words to describe the gratitude I have for all our friends, neighbors and family for their support. To my sisters Julie Arvold and Karen Schuelke, thank you for being such rocks when the bottom fell out, as well as Melanie Schei and the YaYa's. Sandy Jenniges, you will always have a place in my heart. I would like to especially thank Mavis and Sid Boushek for the important research they did regarding Charles Boushek. To Bob and Mary Wetmore, profuse thanks for your kind promotion of my books through A & W Furniture and Gifts. To the many whom I don't have space to list who stood in our corner and through silent care never left, God bless you. Last but not least, I extend my most shining final thanks to the two people who are responsible for the reality of this book: my amazing editor, Emilie Cerar at Resurrection Press and Sister Mary Southard, CSJ, whose magnificent artwork visually embodies the spirit of this book. I celebrate hope with all of you as well as the revelations of love that drench our lives each and every day. Adolfo, here's to everlasting, cool, blue Smoothies.

I am also grateful to the editors of the following publications, in which versions of many chapters of this book were originally published, including:

"The Ten Lessons of Horror" reprinted by permission from *The Light Within: A Women's Book of Solace,* ACTA Publications, Chicago, IL, 2001, page 105.

"Gate Ways to Healing" reprinted by permission from *Meditations For the Bereaved,* Gilgal Publications, © 2002 by Gilgal Publications, P.O. Box 3399, Sunriver, OR 97707.

"Lifter of Our Hearts" which appears as On the Doorstep of Our Hearts—Reprinted by permission from the National Catholic Reporter, August 24, 2001. *NCR.*

"Names of God"—originally appeared in Catholic Women's Network, June/July/August 2001 issue.

"A Million Brushing Wings," which appeared as "Stars on the Blackest Night" reprinted by permission from The National Catholic Reporter, December 8, 2000, *NCR.*

"Woman's Song." reprinted by permission from Woman's Song of Peace card, LaGrange Ministry of the Arts, La Grange, Pk. IL, 1995.

"An Empty Nest and Beyond" reprinted by permission from *The Light Within: A Woman's Book of Solace,* ACTA Publications, Chicago, IL, 2001, page 36.

"They Dwelt Among Us and Still Do" which appeared as "Home in Annie's Sacred Space," reprinted by permission from The National Catholic Reporter, February 8, 2002, *NCR.*

"Mic's Message—Two Years Later" which appeared as "Survivors Support Survivors on the Web," reprinted by permission from the National Catholic Reporter, September 7, 2001, *NCR.*

"The Circle of Life" reprinted by permission from Catholic Women's Network, June/July/August, 2002.

Preface

WHEN my sister's young son, Jamie, was about three years old, he had trouble sleeping because his biological clock always woke him up just before the crack of dawn. Filled with passion, he would wake up energetic and ready to face the day—long before the rest of the family was ready to open their eyes. My sister thought that if she put black-out shades on my nephew's window, he would not wake up so early. However, the next morning, even though his room was completely dark, he woke up at the crack of dawn anyway, and went racing into the living room, calling in delight, "it's morning in the living room!" where indeed, he could see the sun rising over the lake and streaming into the house.

The story touched me and I immediately saw parallels in it relating to the inner vision I experienced following the death of our son by probable suicide. Sometimes we just know things in our hearts, and even though we may be experiencing a horrendously dark time, a spiritual voice in us knows that somewhere deep down—in some mysterious place within us—there is a sunlit place waiting for us. This book traces my journey to finding that "morning in the living room" following the wrenching loss of our son, when it felt as if black-out shades had been drawn permanently.

The commonality that those who have lost loved ones to suicide share when they are immersed in sorrow is the potential for greater vision into the meaning of life, oneself, others and God. Like the author of the book of Revelations, we initially feel as if we are cast onto the rocky island of Patmos, where wind-driven waves batter the shoreline. Yet, like John, during times of desolation, we learn to look beyond that which we see with our eyes; we discover (as my young nephew instinctively knew) that the confined, dark space we are in opens into wider, panoramic vistas just beyond our present horizon. With time and healing, we find that, like "stepping into the morning in the living room," powerful, unfolding truths wait for us that will bring us comfort and peace. These things flood us with moments of brilliance when we least expect it, encouraging us to take heart. Like John, who did not ask for his visions, our inner revelations, while "ordinary" in the sacred sense of the word, also come with clarity and insight that strengthen and uplift us, paving the way for renewed purpose and passion in life.

The only requirement for receiving their messages is that we be receptive. Opening does not happen all at once, but little by little, as we unblock and unlock our grief-torn hearts, allowing hope a chance to gently seep in. It takes patience, time and nurturing care to allow ourselves to believe in life again; yet it is within that vulnerability of our reaching that God surrounds us with support, befriends us and helps us to feel safe, whole and vital again. It is my hope that this book will serve as an emissary to those who are enmeshed in the tragedy of losing a loved one to suicide—a reminder that there's life beyond the black-out shades where Divine Compassion invites us into the sun-fused living room of God's heart. As we learn to redefine ourselves and start life over, it is here that we ultimately understand that beyond the lessons we learn from experiencing such unspeakable loss lies *the gift of recognition*—of the spiritual world that is, was and always will be.

Joni Woelfel

I

How Shall We Live?

*"Choose life so that you and your descendants may live,
loving the Lord your God… and holding fast to him; for
that means life to you and length of days . . ."*
Deuteronomy 30:19b, 20a.

*In the beginning, all we can do is keep remembering that
faith is as powerful and limitless as grief, our response matters, prayer is optional and above all, we must help each other
keep our hearts safe. We can learn to give ourselves a second
chance, even if our loved one did not. Even in death, life
and love hold out their hands to us.*

1

༄ Changed Forever ༄

We know that all things work together for good for those
who love God, Who are called according to his purpose.

Romans 8:28

FOR me, one of the most significant things that happened following our son's death was when I called the local newspaper that I write for and asked them to interview us. I felt a fierce protection of our son when I found out that suicide isn't generally covered by newspapers and therefore, the life of the person isn't celebrated publicly. It never occurred to us to have shame, but we discovered that there is sometimes a dark-ages mentality, silence and taboo surrounding the topic of suicide. The publishers I contacted said they wanted to interview us and the next day their editor spent at least an hour with us listening and asking caring questions and later met with some of our son's friends. She wanted to know what the suicide experience was like for us, what messages we had for others to help educate them and to help us celebrate our son's life publicly. I felt my heart would burst with love, sorrow and pride from the things my family shared. Even though we were still extremely traumatized, this was our first experience in being proactive in our grief, our first inkling in realizing how profoundly altered and changed we would be as a family and as individuals.

In a short time, I memorized the statistics by heart: *suicide is the second leading cause of death in children, teens and young adults. Every year, about 30,000 people in the United States of all ages, ethnic and racial groups die by suicide. Suicide is the eighth leading cause of death overall, with white men aged 65 and over having the highest rate. For every completed suicide there is an average of 8 close survivors, meaning that nearly 7 million people across the country have survived the suicide death of a loved one.*[1] I kept repeating them to myself, unable to comprehend the magnitude of those numbers and filled with disbelief that our dear son was now a face of suicide. I did not think my heart could bear it.

Somehow I made a private Holy Hour on the Saturday morning—one week to the day that our son died. I watched the clock, noting the time he had passed over—about 10:30. It was the most wrenching thing I've ever done, but I wanted to do it for our son's sake and for my own. Even though I was trembling with grief, there was a gentleness that evolved through the relived horror as I tried to bring a mother's love to Mic during the last hour of his life. I talked to him for two hours, said everything I needed to say from my heart, leaving nothing out. When I was done, I left candles burning the rest of the day, letting them usher in that illusive, flickering First Peace and the knowledge that God alone would be able to get us through this.

Before I made the Holy Hour, I had been trying to carry the whole horror on my shoulders and in my mind, constantly trying to connect with, understand and enter into that dark night of the soul when everything unraveled for our son. I was agitated in spirit in a way that defied description, feeling bleak, forlorn and like Jesus did in the Garden of Gethsemane when he had cried out to God, "Why have you forsaken me?" (Gethsemane means "wine press," very fitting since we feel as if we've been drained of our very essence when there.)

Following my prayer vigil, I felt relieved about details I would never be able to know, as if God was reminding me firmly, *"This knowledge is for me to carry, not you."* After that, although it was extremely difficult, I began trying not to keep reliving the events that couldn't be explained or that changed that fateful night before and the morning our son died. As my middle son, Dana said, "We are still an intact family. We are still three boys (and two girls, referring to our son's life partners). We are still an unbroken circle of love with Mic in the middle." Those words were tested and challenged time and time again, as we each grieved in our own ways. But despite our inability to always be there for one another, love was pulling us forward. What we didn't realize was that the six of us, each in our own way, was being offered something secret and priceless . . . called the Legacy of Grief, that would change us forever.

God of Mysteries and Deeply Concealed Treasures, in Your own time, when we are ready, You call us forth to new ways, new days, new clarity and new passion.

2

❧ The Beginning: Early Promises ❧

I will appoint Peace as your overseer.   Isaiah 60:17b

AT 8:20 on Monday morning, I wrote, "Our son has now been dead for one week and two days. This is the first time I have been alone in my house or had the strength to come to the computer. My heart feels as if it has literally shattered into a million pieces that rolled through the cracks in the floor. Sleep brings reprieve but nightmares awaken us to dread and lower level panic. We hate to go to bed because then we are alone with our unbearable thoughts, and we hate to wake up because reality crashes us as if upon the rocks of some unidentifiable, ocean-bashed island. We never knew the human soul could know such rawness."

Especially during the first five days, I was afraid to be by myself. I kept imagining a cocoon, a place of safety, needing to be alone yet afraid to be. The first image came to me just two hours after we knew of our son's death. The sheriff had left (and for the first time, I had spoken of our beloved boy in the past tense) and our home was filled with the sobbing of our son's friends, our family and neighbors. I was lying on my bed and suddenly I had a mystical experience in my imagination. Our son had entered my womb spiritually, as an embryo. I imaged my spirit enfolding and completely encircling the embryo. I knew it was my broken heart speaking the only language it knew, offering the embryo as the symbol of the new life he now lived . . . yet still mysteriously a part of my spirit forever.

The next day, while lying on my bed meditating again, I had a brief sense of our son being close beside me. I imagined stroking his bristly crew cut, and saying softly, "It's OK, Honey, go and be free, Mom understands." (Meaning I knew that he wasn't thinking like himself and had made a fatal, tragic mistake that he would take back, if he could.) I never once felt that his spirit was afraid, lost or anxious. If I had one gift, it was the constant, inexplicable feeling of reassurance that he was OK. I said to people, "I know our son is OK, but we (his family) are the ones who are not OK."

The sense of unreality during those first weeks was profound. I could never remember what day it was or even the month. The first sign of healing—believing I could survive our son's death—was when a kind priest held my hand and said, "Suicide is an illness. Don't try to understand it now, it can't be fully understood; never blame or judge yourself because there is only one compassionate judge, God." This early love shown to us changed the course of my grief. It was like it curved into a different stream of consciousness. The poignancy of sharing this grief with our son's friends went beyond words. Traumatized, they came to us those first days, needing to be here. Our house seemed filled with purity and light and I imagined our son lingering here and there, just drifting and moving serenely from place to place and person to person.

Who will we become? I asked. How will we survive this? My heart became an island of tears that I felt would never know an end.

God of Early Grief, when we have no capacity for comprehension and even when we flat out wouldn't believe it anyway, You make a promise that holds on to us: Peace will come.

3

✤ Why? ✤

"That which is, is far off, and deep, very deep, who can find it out?"   Ecclesiastes 7:24

ONE time, in a grief support group I was in, a father who had lost a teenage son to suicide asked in anguish, "Why? Why would he do it?" A beautiful young college girl who was in the group said compassionately, reaching out to the bereft father, "I am sorry to hear about your son, but it sounds like he was a terrific child, with a very loving and caring family. I suffer from depression and please know that it's not anything that any of you (or your family) did that made your son take his own life. For me anyway, there isn't one thing that makes me depressed; it's all of the little things that shouldn't matter that I let get to me, and in the long run it ends up bringing me down until I just crash . . ."

Sharon Allard writes in her unpublished manuscript *Within These Walls*[2] about her journey with depression, ". . . We live in a world of walls. Walls surround us, shelter us, protect us. They can be used for support or to enclose or divide. A small word, a simple concept, but oh, the strength of a wall. I am a wall builder. At some point in time, my walls started to crumble . . ." Allard, a respected ICU nurse, continued, "The sun was brilliant that day as I drove along the narrow winding road up to the mountain. On one side were enormous rock cliffs and on the other was a breathtaking panorama as the desert and the city stretched out far below me. I found the spot I was looking for, a place I had already visited, had picked out carefully in fact, several months before. The road jutted out in a hairpin curve, the edge dropping off into nearly a thousand feet of cacti and boulders. I stopped the car and looked around. For a long time, I watched a small lizard on the rock face across from me, climbing, skittering, first up, then down, then sideways.

"I thought about my reason for this trip up to the mountain. I thought of my husband and children. I pictured their faces, heard their voices in my mind and ached for them in my heart. I wondered what it would be like for them afterwards, for I had made my trip on this beautiful day for only one reason. I planned to drive over the edge of the mountain and kill myself. Over the previous year, I had become more and more depressed, I became more 'burned out' and my sense of uselessness increased until I had driven up the mountain to find a place to die when I could no longer handle my life. There were people who loved me. My family certainly did. I knew I needed help, but it seemed so complicated. Deep down, I think I knew I was soul-sick with an undefined 'I-don't-know-what' . . . even God seemed distant. I climbed and skittered this way and that, like the lizard, so small and insignificant. I retreated into the cold, dark hell of my walls. I even told myself God would understand. I realized that I wasn't really scared, and the thought occurred to me that I was not afraid to die—but rather to live."

Allard's revealing, poetic words bring insight into the world of a seriously depressed person. While she went on to work with a wonderful therapist and found her way, many just as valiant as she is, do not survive. (The Journal of the American Medical Association has reported that 95% of all suicides occur at the peak of a depressive episode.[3] Depressive illnesses can distort a person's thinking, so that they don't think clearly or rationally. They may not know they have a treatable illness, or they think they can't be helped.) As Adina Wrobleski writes in her book, *Suicide: Survivors, A Guide For Those Left Behind,* "There are two aspects of the question "Why?" The first we can know; that is, "Why did they die?" The simple, but truthful answer is that the person we loved so much got so sick (usually with depression) that they died, and the way someone dies from depression is by suicide. The chemicals in their brains that affected how they thought, felt and behaved were out of balance, causing them to view the future and their world as places they could no longer live in—places that were too painful to live in. On the day that my daughter killed herself, what made her decide after lunch that 'now' was the time when absolutely all hope was gone? That is the 'why' I will never know." [4]

Compassionate, Embracing God of the Ones Who Did Not Make it, comfort and remind those left behind that it is love, joy and eternal life that defines the present world of our loved ones who passed over and not one tragic moment in time when defenses did not hold.

4

✥ An Unfailing Net ✥

. . . take me out of the net that is hidden for me, for you
are my refuge. . . . in the shelter of your presence . . . you
hold them safe . . .   Psalm 31:4, 20a, b

ONE of the universal statements often made by the newly
bereaved who have lost loved ones to suicide is: *They
didn't love me enough to stay.* Understandably, this uneducated
concept is expressed in despair, futility or shame and sometimes
in desolation—in the case of children who have lost a parent to
suicide. To see their initial sense of betrayal and abandonment is
especially wrenching. Another anguishing worry commonly
expressed is a spiritual one: *My loved one killed himself and now
won't be able to go to heaven.*

Well-known author of the book *The Pummeled Heart,* Antoinette
Bosco, who lost a beloved son to suicide, addresses both of these
issues powerfully in her writing, "My son was an achiever, popular
with all who went to school with him, worked with him, dealt with
him in any way. A graduate of a well-known university, he was a
math teacher and the author of three books, all before he was
twenty-seven. Yet, he took his life, telling us, 'Something is missing
. . . my life is like a Rolls Royce without spark plugs. It looks great,
but it has a hidden flaw that keeps it from running properly. The
absence of that spark has often made even the simplest setbacks for
me almost unendurable . . .'[5] Before this special person took his
life, he left behind several notes and a lengthy, taped message to

help his family understand. His doing this has comforted his mother immensely and as a gift to others, she offers what he said in order that they, too, might be comforted.

Antoinette continues, "What comes through in my son's tape is his tormenting struggle to survive in those times when he was not fully equipped to handle life as it must be lived on this earth. Something in the essential mechanism that one needs to be able to greet—and not just endure—each day was missing, and it gave him unrelenting and unbearable pain. The American Association of Suicidology has coined a word to express this: psych-ache. I feel that this pain, perhaps is what defeats most young adults who . . . are not on a self-destructive path and yet kill themselves. They don't really want to die. They want to live, but they don't have the 'spark plugs' that could save them. Most are highly intelligent, with attractive personalities, creative and outgoing, sensitive, dedicated and deeply concerned for others. They're also very good at hiding their pathological breakdowns—a frightening inner turmoil that quietly erupts all too frequently, but is under control until something devastatingly dramatic happens. That then shatters the connection to their carefully crafted safety nets, and they want out of this life. In one of the notes my son left me, he said it was 'time to go home.' He was telling me he killed himself in the hopes of finding a better life, one without the missing parts and indescribable pain."

She remembers, "We didn't have a clue that my son was moving away from us. Knowing we'd be shocked by his chosen death, he tried to help us by asking, in one of his notes, that we, family and friends, have a gathering—not for 'a time of mourning but a time of healing. Lay my spirit to rest.' And he underscored, 'Feel no guilt, for there is no fault.'" Antoinette also adds, "What also comforts me is that the church now shows compassion for people like my son and others who die by suicide, as the *Catechism of the Catholic Church* makes clear: 'We should not despair of the eternal salvation of persons who take their own lives . . .' " (2282-83).

Through the enlightenment offered by Antoinette and the beautiful legacy of her son, we are reminded that lack of love is rarely, if ever, what suicide is about.

God Who Catches Us When the Bottom Drops Out, we are all—every single one of us—safely upheld in the unfailing net of Your protective presence, in this world and the next.

5

ༀ Passion Incarnate ༀ
Sharing the Pain

Set me as a seal upon your heart,
for love is strong as death
passion fierce as the grave.
Song of Songs 8:6

IT'S ironic, how sometimes a small, seemingly insignificant
question can be the key to opening a whole new universe of
insights that one had never considered before. This happened for
me, when early on in my grief, I asked my friends who have lost
children, *"When the human spirit is gifted with insight and vision for
living, does this expanded way of looking at life produce passion? Does
it seem possible to say that suffering-vision-passion go hand in hand?"*

Antoinette Bosco, author of the award-winning book *Choosing
Mercy,* who has not only lost one son to suicide but a son and
daughter-in-law to murder said, "As for the differences, if any,
between suffering and passion, I think there is a great one.
Suffering is often thrust upon us by a hard event, like a death or an
accident or an illness. We must learn to cope with this and transform it. Passion is not thrust upon us. It is a choice. We become
passionate for a better world, for a new sense of the wonder of creation, for an enraptured sense of the mystery of our own creation—
and now, filled with passion, we can let the suffering go and bring
a new life to the world."

Adolfo Quezada, therapist and author of *Heart Peace* agreed, writing in a powerful statement, "Passion is the energy of God moving through us. It may take the form of immeasurable joy or horrific suffering, both the stuff of life." Lillian Meyers, a psychologist who is active in Compassionate Friends introduced the word *inspiration*. "I have a certain passion for life that I believe is a commitment for what you believe in deeply," she said. "I recognize and accept the 'gifts' of grief, about which I am passionate and use to reach out to give hope and support to the bereaved, the abandoned, the stigmatized and the excluded." Lillian included a poem by Robert Hamilton: "I walked a mile with Pleasure, she chattered all the way, but I was none the wiser, for all she had to say; I walked a mile with Sorrow, ne'er a word said she, but oh, the things I learned from her—when Sorrow walked with me."

Judy Osgood, publisher of Gilgal books for the grieving, wrapped everyone's words up in love, as she wrote about the death of her son and a visit to church. Poignantly describing the moment, Judy described a prayer service in which, for the first time, she fully realized that Mary, Jesus and God felt pain and shared our human emotions. "I recognized for the first time what asking Jesus to die for us cost our Heavenly Father," she wrote. "My whole being wept that night for God, for Jesus, for Mary until I could cry no more, and I have never been the same since. In light of that extraordinary experience, I see *passion*, first and foremost, *as a love that transcends human emotions*. It was love that enabled Jesus to sacrifice Himself for us and that sacrifice adds another layer of meaning to the word. And finally, I see it as a driving force that enabled Him to do so."

The powerful, tender words and diverse journeys of each of these writers brought to mind a passage from a biography of Thomas Merton by Monica Furlong. She wrote, "Somehow between 1955 and 1960, Merton became, painfully and slowly, 'his own man,' no longer believing that anyone else 'knew best' but seeking and questioning for himself with a new energy. Scales seemed to fall from his eyes, and the world and its people . . . were suddenly flooded with beauty and meaning." [6] To me, this illustrates when Passion Incarnate, known as *Akme,* "the moment of truth," becomes reality to us. Like the people who responded to my query, the grief transformed shines forth from their eyes, their words, their work and their dedication.

Prayer: God who is the Pulse of Love and Meaningful Living, thank You for being the energy that urges us to reclaim our passion and purpose from the inside out.

6

⚜ Sacrifice of Coals ⚜
Releasing Negative Emotions

And I said: "Woe is me! I am lost . . . Then one of the seraphs flew to me, holding a live coal . . .

Isaiah 6: 5a, 6a

DURING the grief journey, survivors of suicide often encounter experiences of feeling betrayed by those who make callous judgments, or even toward the loved one who committed suicide. Once, I wrote a story about a pilgrim whose spirit was ill because of betrayal. The pilgrim, no matter where she went, felt homeless, like she didn't belong anywhere. She kept having dreams of crossroads, where she would come to forks in the road and not know which way to turn. No direction seemed right, no companion seemed right, no place seemed right, and so finally, feeling she could not go on, she found a cave in a nearby mountain and moved in. In the story, she needed the cave because it was safe from the elements and provided shelter. It was a solitary place that granted comfort, but it did not bring healing to her heart. She could not forget searing words that, in her mind, shattered her world and all she held sacred. She did not know how to move on or redefine herself after the betrayal that radically changed how she understood the very foundations of life.

Finally, in the middle of the night, an angel appeared to her in her dreams. The pilgrim cried, "Please give me advice, tell me what to do . . . for I feel completely alone and have lost my way. I am

27

trapped in uncertainty and hopelessness." The angel spread white, shimmering wings above the pilgrim, saying gently, "You are traumatized by too many bad things that have happened to you. You do not see the true perspective because these things have made your spirit ill." Tears streamed down the pilgrim's face as she said, "But, I don't know what to do about it. I feel like my heart is hollow." The angel bent her wings in an enfolding manner and said, "Your spirit is ill because important things that should have held didn't, and people in whom you trusted have failed you. This pattern of betrayal has warped and wounded your perceptions and now because of it, you must learn the most powerful lesson a human being can learn: *there is no lasting security or peace except in God.* This is not what you want to hear because it requires such faith. And, when you are ill in your spirit, resilience and faith while still present, do not serve you because you have lost the ability to lean on them. Yet, in reality, these are the two things that save and carry you when your heart is broken.

The angel continued, "Rely on unseen forces, for these are your strength. Rise and face the truth in your heart. Release unexpressed emotions that are withering your spirit." In the dream, the angel gave the pilgrim a basket of black coals. With a mystical gesture of her hand, the angel brought to life a small bonfire at the pilgrim's feet. "Call forth your honest feelings," the angel instructed, and one by one, as you name them, throw them into the fire. The pilgrim, feeling compelled by the angel's suggestion, selected the biggest and blackest coal and grasping it in her fist, gripped it, unable to let it go. The angel said with compassion, "Take your time, the first one is always the hardest. Hold onto it and let it speak to you." The pilgrim kneaded the coal, knowing it was blackening her palm in doing so. Suddenly, she saw an image of her inner heart, infused with black blemishes. A single phrase rose to her lips and she said it aloud: Desire for Retribution. She hurled the coal into the fire. The angel nodded in encouragement. "This is like giving birth," she said, "the labor will be painful and wrenching but you can do it. Your heart knows what needs to be released." The pilgrim was grimacing as she recalled crushing memories, and as she did so, uttered two more stinging words: rage and undeserved. "Righteous anger is healing," the angel said. "Release the unfair experiences life and other people have brought you."

Within an hour, the basket of coals was empty as one by one, the pilgrim had expressed her sorrow, pain and inertia. The fire grew so large with the sacrifice of coals that the pilgrim did not even realize that the fire consumed her and she was engulfed in living flame that did not burn or harm. Standing within the ashes of what was formerly her life as she knew it, the angel said softly as the dream faded, "let the betrayal in your life serve as the ignition for the flames of wisdom, justice and forgiveness. Let the fire of faith free you and usher in a completely new life that blesses."

Crossroads God of Living Comfort, thank You for reassuring us that You, heavenly hosts of all manner and the spirits of our beloved who have crossed over hover near, encouraging and helping us when we need to heal and move forward in life.

7

❧ An Important Message ❧
At the Cemetery

As a mother comforts her child, so I will comfort you.

Isaiah 66:13

ONE Indian summer day, I wrote, "Our son has now been gone one month and five days. Last week the "If onlys" and the "What did I do wrongs" set in like a beast, interweaving with the knowledge that we were good parents as I recounted all the loving gestures, memories and words. We mourn because we were not allowed to say goodbye or I love you. We have anger because we are left with such emptiness and the physical ache of arms that want to hold him and grasp only air."

We wept on the day that would have been our son's last day of work, his first day back at school, the first dance all his friends went to without him, the fact that it was chilly and we couldn't remind him to wear his jacket. We were still programmed to nurture and protect him in our heart of hearts, but he was no longer there. We were a wounded family. Nearly every day, it seemed, someone told us of someone they knew or heard of, usually a teenager, who committed suicide. That fall was to have been one of the best times in our lives. Each of us had goals and dreams coming true, we had overcome significant family hardships; this was supposed to be and would have been our family's Golden Time. We had worked so hard for it.

Now instead, we found ourselves starting life over from scratch, always feeling the presence of our son's absence. We tried to help each other keep our hearts safe. In the meantime, we remembered when our son was still alive and filling our lives with his unique wonder of life. No one loved falling leaves, wind, morning sunrises, the moon, the call of a Canadian goose more than he did. We had tears in our eyes not only because of pain now, but because of the utter piercing beauty in the change of seasons as it transformed the village we live in. All the while, it was the landscape of our souls that was changing the most.

My grief was like a vast and winding canyon, a seemingly impassable chasm. I had experiences that caused me to take sharp turns that kept redefining the grief. A significant landmark in this process was the day I went to the cemetery and place of death for the first time. I'd been waiting for the time when I felt that it was right . . . and that day it snowed huge, gentle snowflakes all day— the size of silver dollars. Going to the place of death felt like a "thin" place where the spirit world was especially close while the snow shrouded everything in a screen of white. Our son had chosen a wild, tall-grassed place on a beautiful curve on the river that bordered a cornfield to die. Two white crosses marked the exact spot where he was found. The untamed beauty of the spot (beloved and familiar to him) seemed to hold a sense of his spirit even though we believed he had gone to a happy place.

I recalled Matthew 11:28, "Come to me, all you that are weary and carrying heavy burdens, and I will give you rest," and how Joyce Rupp paraphrased it in *Your Sorrow is My Sorrow,* "I lean my burdened life on the bosom of your love and wait to be consoled." [7] This helped me to understand Mic's mindset at the time—like he couldn't go on and had decided to lay his life down on the bosom of that beloved place.

It was only later that I learned that most people who die by suicide have unrecognized, untreated and undiagnosed depression or anxiety disorders, that, like cancer or heart disease, can result in death. *Suicide was not a choice our son made,* but something he considered his only option because he was not well in his thinking at the time. Healthy people do not kill themselves and I knew in my heart that our son would never have left us had he been himself. Somehow this knowledge consoled me and I felt it was a message he wanted all of us to receive. I began to feel as if I was within our son's eternal heart rather than him being within mine, as I began that early, wrenching journey to understanding *why.*

The gentle dollops of snow filled my hair and settled on my shoulders silently, almost as if they were floating, suspending me in time and space, insulating me with love and carrying a message of consolation and a glimpse of peace.

God Who Knows Exactly What Our Souls Need and Exactly When, sometimes all You say is "Hush, be quiet . . . just be and let Me do the rest."

8

✣ The Way of the Maze ✣
The Gift of Tears

. . . by a road they do not know, by paths they have not known I will guide them. I will turn . . . the rough places into level ground . . . and I will not forsake them.

Isaiah 42:16

YOU could have heard a pin drop. My husband was reading the Intercessory Prayers of Petition at the podium during Mass. When he came to the place asking for prayers for a local sixteen-year-old girl who had been killed in a car accident the day before, he broke down for a minute as he struggled to regain composure. As an experienced lector, he did not expect this sudden flood of emotion; it just happened. Looking out over the congregation, he could see friends and neighbors crying. Just seven weeks before, our own son had died. The beautiful young girl who died was a classmate of our son's. My husband wept for the fragileness of life, the loss of children and the knowledge of what it is like to wake up each morning facing the finality of knowing you will never see that smiling face again in this life.

After Mass, a woman who had tragically lost a child years ago spoke with my husband saying gently, *"It is a gift for people to see emotion and grieving;* we don't need to be ashamed of our tears." At home, after my husband and I spoke of the event, I patted his cheek tenderly, saying, "It is so hard to be a gift, isn't it?" In my diary, I wrote, "Even in our tragedies, it seems we are offered this option: we can be a gift or we can choose not to be. But, the greatest comfort comes, when we say yes."

For many people like us, passing into the new millennium meant carrying an ark of sorrow with us. In my mind, it paralleled the exodus of the Jews, who, upon leaving Egypt for the promised land carried the ark of the covenant reverently with them on an unknown, rough road. Sorrow is sacred to the bearer; it goes with each of us into the future because the memory of it is ingrained into our hearts and souls by the experiences and losses we have in life.

Even though we carry this sorrow, we awaken each day knowing there is a choice that can be made between despair and faith. I liken this choice to the image of a maze. A maze is full of paths, twists and turns, and sometimes, we come upon those dead ends. These dead ends are what despair is like. When we encounter them, we need to make a choice to turn around and backtrack a bit; and then take a different inner path that will bring us to the avenues of hope and comfort again. Memories of terror and the pangs of grief which cause us to feel as if we can't go on are like coming up against that dead end wall in a maze or blind alley. We feel as if our breath has been knocked out of us and we are entangled in barbed wire. Eventually, as time goes on and we begin healing, we become Street Smart. Even though we may be wounded and battered, we learn the Way of the Maze. We know enough to turn around when we hit the wall of despair and like my husband, as we move forward again, *allow our tears and sorrow to become revelations of love.*

God Who Knows the Way Out, when we don't know where we're going, You do. You do not lead us through an unending, meaningless maze of tears following a loved one's death by suicide; You guide us to a path of peace, passion and purpose that takes us where we need to go. Without fail Your love guides us and shelters the way.

9

❧ Believe without Seeing ❧

. . . the deep gave forth its voice. The sun raised high its hands. Habakkuk 3:10b

AS the grief process deepens, our moods often feel murky, indistinct and mindless as we become worn out from all the heartache we are carrying. Many years ago I wrote a children's fantasy story about a sunflower who, despite hail, battering wind, drought and storm always faced the sun, which personified God. In the story, the sunflower managed to retain her faith no matter what happened, turning to follow the journey of the sun's trek across the sky each day, even when her leaves turned brown and fell off. Without fail, she trustingly faced the sun during significant and dramatic adversity.

However, one day something unexpected happened in the story that nearly caused the sunflower to lose her way. The sun disappeared from sight, replaced by a shadow that passed overhead and came to stay. The sun was blocked from view and no matter where the sunflower turned, she could not find it. In her mind, a sunflower without the sun was "nothing." The days passed and the shadow not only did not leave but loomed bigger and darker, until one day, the sunflower called out in desperation, "Who are you?" The answer came immediately, "the Shadow of Nothing." The sunflower countered, "What do I have to do to get rid of you?" The wily shadow offered an awful riddle that went like this:

When the sun is gone
And is nowhere to be found,
There's a shift one must do

36

With their heart and not their eyes
Then, all will be fine . . .
If you know the answer, to this rhyme.

Day and night the despondent sunflower begged for a hint, which the shadow answered by retorting, "There's no getting away from me!" But then, one morning, before the shadow was awake, the sunflower heard a mysterious whisper that said, "Believe without seeing." The sunflower understood this revelation immediately and cried, "It's the sun! I believe in you, sun, I believe!" The shadow began immediately dissipating, calling angrily as he disappeared into thin air, "You guessed the riddle! I'll be *baackkkkk* . . ." The sunflower called after him, "Not to stay, you won't!" Later, the sun asked the sunflower, "How could you ever think that I would abandon you?" The sunflower replied in a pensive voice, "Because I couldn't see you." The sun's only reply to the whole matter was, "Let this be a lesson to you."

Twenty years later as I read that simple, innocent but powerful fable, I found I had an important phrase to add to it which was a hallmark of the deepening days following the death of our son. For anyone immersed in a tragedy, there are going to be days when your mind is a turmoil of conflicting thoughts that seem to go nowhere and bring no light or comfort. During times like this when our consciousness needs to heal from the trauma, we are temporarily beyond reasoning. In this shadowed place where nothing makes sense and we can't think straight, God comes to us like he did the sunflower, bending close to our battered hearts and saying, *"Believe without thinking."*

God Who Never leaves us Comfortless, thank You for reminding us that faith is a matter of Your spirit and abiding love within us . . . and not what the mind is capable—or not capable—of contemplating. Let this be a lesson to us.

10

❧ I Believe ☙

". . . and the peace of God, which surpasses all under-standing, will guard your hearts and minds in Christ Jesus. Finally, beloved, whatever is true, whatever is honorable, whatever is just, whatever is pure, whatever is pleasing, whatever is commendable . . . think about these things.   Philippians 4:7, 8

BELIEF is a living, breathing life source that changes and evolves as we do. When we lose a loved one to suicide, we question everything we held as sacred. Terror and despair can make our faith feel like it is turned upside down and dragged through the mud. Many not only feel that they have lost their identity but their faith as well. There is an overwhelming sense of the unknown that affects survivors on all levels—emotionally, psychologically and spiritually. As time goes on, some find that it helps to write down their beliefs—as an affirming thing to lean. These unfolding written faith statements remind us of where our strengths lie. I wrote my belief statements down in a notebook; when I was done, I shared it with loved ones as my personal legacy of faith. It was powerful to me because not only was it written out of the most difficult journey I had ever made but because I viewed it as a gift that I hoped others could find comfort in. I wrote:

"I believe that the power of finding one's voice, expressing it and having it validated is one of the greatest gifts of grief. I believe in consolation, courage, creativity and compassion. I believe that after we die, one of the first things we will be asked is, 'Whom did you comfort?' I believe in synchronicity, authenticity, and intuition. I believe in study, growth, deepening and transformation. I believe in warmth, respecting sacred space and boundaries. I believe in empowerment, honoring the earth and the soul-enlarging properties of humor and integrity. I believe that among the nicest words we can say to another person are, 'You inspire me.' I believe in being wild in the true sense of the word, untamed by the words, 'You should do this or be that.' I believe in children, old people, fat people, bald people, skinny people and tending sick animals.

"I believe in eternal life, common sense and understanding how our life experiences shape who we are. I believe in the healing of scars and trusting that God and our loved ones who have died still weave love into our lives. I believe in embracing human frailty, the power of light and the hope of survival on all levels. I believe in valuing all feelings, including the anger of grief and seeking to understand it rather than naming it a bad emotion. I cannot live my life without believing in happiness. I find richness and satisfaction in solitude, work and recreation and believe that the outer frameworks of our lives are just mantles for the inner heart and inner work we do as our grief journey speaks to us. I believe that forgiveness is a skill that can be learned, and I believe in standing up for one's beliefs, values and ideals. I believe in communication and the importance of listening and waiting with people who grieve. I don't particularly believe in unsolicited advice. I do believe in having mentors (and being one), seeking counsel when it is needed and being grounded in wisdom, patience and self-control.

"I believe in friendship, family, dignity, enfolding and accepting one's limitations and treating all people as equals. I believe in tolerance and taking a risk now and then. I believe that the human body is an earth garment that houses our magnificent, eternal spirits. I believe in the fierceness of passion, tenderness and the politeness of good manners. I believe that we are each here for a purpose and that we cross each other's paths for a reason. I believe in learning from mistakes, in generosity, humility, self-confidence, self-care and being comfortable with the words, 'I don't know.' I believe in wind, curves, openness to new ideas and taking the back roads home. I believe all these 'beliefs' are my highest aspirations, but that they are never perfected in any human being. I believe that, if we practice mindfulness we can lean toward them, rather than away from them, always flowing with a sacred rhythm that will carry us through our grief. Lastly, *I believe in the Peace that Surpasses All Human Understanding with all my heart.*"

God Who Inspires Our Belief, never let us forget that You protect, nourish and cherish our faith in You with all Your heart.

11

⚘ The Ten Lessons of Horror ⚘

I have a hope in God . . . that there will be a resurrec-
tion.   Acts 24:15

T HE spirituality of horror is not something most of us are
   trained in. We do not plan for experiences that will broad-
side us like a monsoon, body-slamming us with terror and sweeping out to sea every foundation we ever believed in. The initial
impact of horror begins with shock, as dazed, we try to comprehend what has 'hit' us.

Before Jesus rose from the dead, the curtain in the sanctuary
was torn in two. This is how many survivors of suicide initially feel:
as if a veil of protection in our lives was ripped in half. Here lies *the*
first lesson in the spirituality of horror. We lose the sense of feeling
safe. With this comes post-traumatic stress that sears like bolts of
lightening. We learn that there is no emotion considered inappro-
priate or abnormal: depression, nightmares, inability to sleep, feeling insane and despondent. As we become well acquainted with
these companions, we learn *the second lesson*: we can tolerate them
because they are a part of the etiology of horror. We are becoming
educated in the landscape of life ravaged by trauma.

The third lesson comes with the first tentative tendrils of explor-
ing why. How could this happen? How could our loved one have
done what they did? All we have are questions, self blame and no
answers that make any sort of sense. This brings us to *the fourth les-*
son: it is OK not to have answers. As more time passes we find we

41

are at least acting normal and smiling in the right places when people talk to us. Grace enables us to go through the motions. The first signs of comfort rise with the ability to physically function as we return to work, responsibilities and embracing those we care about. Without even realizing it, we have progressed to *lesson number five:* We find that reaching out to others is life giving and that we are actually able to do it. More comfort weaves its way into our lives, but with it comes setbacks. *Lesson number six:* flashbacks occur and we reel with the finality that our loved one is gone. Our eyes may be dry but our hearts continue to sob as we sink into bleak truth, knowing healing won't come without doing this. We begin floating with this rhythm.

By now, we know that few can truly understand our journey who haven't been there. Those who have not known horror have begun distancing themselves and we find this is often best for all of us. We begin gathering in, letting go and no longer needing to devour grief books. Book learning helped at first, but now, we are beginning to live our grief . . . not study and define it. *Lesson seven* teaches us that our grief is a part of us that will always be there. We also sense that it will evolve but we find peace accepting the fact that we won't be able to figure out where it will take us ahead of time. The blame we may have felt has been transformed into an embracing understanding of human frailty. *Lesson eight* brings us the knowledge that God will never fit in a box, but that God and hope are going to find us in time. *Lesson nine* brings the wisdom of tenderness as we come into the fullness of understanding how transient 'things' are and how lasting matters of the heart are. *Lesson ten* brings a promise that we wouldn't have believed when our loved one took their own life: Horror has wounded us but it has not destroyed us. Love is stronger than death and we feel the resurrection of it uplifting and salvaging us every day.

God of Holy Thursday and Good Friday, no one empathizes more than You do, when we feel as if our faith has been to hell and back. Battered and shaken, we learn that resurrection is not only some far off, obscure final happening but a living incarnation of comfort that is with us now, when we need it the most.

12

❧ Gateways to Healing ❧

So again Jesus said to them, very truly, I tell you, I am the gate . . . I come that they may have life and have it abundantly. John 10:7a, 10b

WHEN Mic died, it was as if the very gates of life itself slammed shut. Our family felt that the ability to experience joy, laughter and the appreciation of simple family pleasures without him was lost to us forever. Our other two sons and daughter-in-law—all in college—were grieving deeply; that I knew. It was apparent in their eyes and in the things they didn't say rather than in what they said. The language of their grief was different than my husband's and mine and after an uncomfortable bungle or two, I learned to give them the space they needed and not press them to talk. Instead, I began to read between the lines, to discern voice inflections and to try to let go of feeling I needed to mold or "guide" them in their grief. While they were subtle in what they shared, I knew that besides profound sadness, they felt some initial betrayal and anger. One son confided that he felt cheated because all the dreams and future happy times of hunting, golfing and fishing together were snatched away. Mic's choice was not his older brothers' and sister-in-law's choice. They, like my husband and I, were heartbroken that we were not consulted or given a chance to extend comfort and resolution to Mic. As a family, we were all left with fractured lives and no chance to even say goodbye.

While we tried to remain connected, our edges nudged one another and it seemed that we needed to travel our grief journeys separately in those early months. I could not see much measurable progress. This troubled me as a mother, because I wanted to fix everything and this couldn't be fixed. Then, my close friend, Judy Osgood wrote me an enlightening letter that changed my perspective completely. She wrote: *"We each have a gate that must be opened and then walked through to come out on the other side of our loss. When we can focus on the makeup of that gate, find the key to unlocking it and then deal with it, we are on our way to healing."* This message marked one of the most defining moments that I've ever had. I began seeing gateways in my two sons' and their partners' lives that had been coming into being all along—invisible but very real, just the same.

The discovery of the presence of those gateways shifted the rhythm of my own grief in many ways. I began to notice that our family's laughter together was not forced for the sake of sparing each other pain but came from spontaneous, light-hearted moments. Our middle son, Dana, who is studying radiology and our daughter-in-law, Jennifer, created a stunning, raised rock grotto and memorial flower bed in the shape of Mic's first initial as a dedication to him. With their little dog, Mowgli, they worked day and night, filled with passion and delight in what they were creating. Our oldest son, Damian, who is studying to be an anthropologist, began making authentic flint knives out of obsidian and deer antlers. You could hear him chipping away in the woods by a campfire, filled with the pride and satisfaction of creativity while his partner, Rachel, read stories aloud from *The Hobbit*. The light in their eyes, the grins, the joking, the life-giving quality of voice inflection all indicated that each had found their gateways. I felt such relief.

One day, I was trying to make a decision about a problem, and I heard Mic's voice in my mind say, "Mom, *it'll be fine,*" the way he always said those words with such endearing friendliness. Later, when the problem was solved, I perceived him saying, *"Sweet . . ."* his trademark remark, as if he were teasing, "I told you so!" While I still felt a tear well up, I also felt warmed inside as I recognized the reality of my own gateway. My son's beautiful voice that resides in my heart was at last coming through and always would be, just as it was for each of us in our family . . . and for every family who has ever lost a loved one.

Divine Gatekeeper of our Hearts, for those who grieve, your healing message reminds us every day: Make no mistake, don't doubt it for a minute . . . the gateway that connects this world with the next is most assuredly there.

13

❧ Best Kept Secrets ❧ Human Intimacy

I am my beloved's and my beloved is mine; I am faint with love.　　　　　　　　Song of Solomon 6:3, 5:8b

"SEXUALITY is an organic, normal, physical and emotional function of human life," writes Christiane Northrup, M.D. in her book, *Women's Bodies, Woman's Wisdom: Creating Physical and Emotional Health and Healing.* "We need to imagine what our sexuality would be like if we thought of it as holy and sacred, a gift from the same source that created the ocean, the waves and the stars," she says. Furthermore, she teaches that "we all have access to the life-force—the erotic, ecstatic energy of our being because it is a part of being human." [8]

When a loved one has been lost to suicide, every aspect of human nature is affected, including the ability and need to give and receive physical love and tenderness through touch. Although it is one of the least talked about issues survivors of suicide face, it is a very important one. In an interview, I asked Sonny, an upstanding young father, how the death of his son to suicide changed his life. He immediately responded with openness and honesty, "As in any good Catholic family, we talked about sex all the time. We talked about it, never did it. Two things happened. First, my wife, who I love very much, and I thought we would never be sexually active again after our son died, because we felt so destroyed. About a month later, one Sunday after church, we went into our bedroom to change clothes and hugged each other. It was like a dam burst and we were intimate. However, at the end, my wife burst into uncontrollable crying. This crying happened every time we were intimate, for a long time. About a week ago, for the first time, she did not cry and I knew it was a good sign that she was healing. She said that at the end of lovemaking, she would start to think about our son who died and how he had not experienced physical love, which is such a beautiful thing to us and that he would never experience it."

The unfolding story of this courageous young couple powerfully expresses the comfort and healing that human sexuality and intimacy can bring; it also reveals the torment that many survivors feel when a loved one has died so young and tragically—without having had a chance to grow up and experience the fullness of life.

In another interview, the story was told of Sophia, a beautiful young teenage girl who lost her brother to suicide. She and her brother were very close, and he was her sounding board and confidant regarding boyfriend problems. When her brother died, the young girl was inconsolable in her grief. Seeking comfort, lonely and depressed, she turned to physical love and intimacy and soon became pregnant and an unwed mother. Her family embraced her completely, understanding why she had looked for love in the wrong places. Through their support, the young girl and her child were nurtured; there were no judgments or accusations, and this valiant family went forward in life, wounded but determined to stay strong and close as a family.

Meredith, a senior citizen confided, "My grief was so consuming, that no words—nothing—could comfort me. It was a very long time before I even realized that my husband and I had stopped touching each other. But one day, when his hand lightly brushed my hair affectionately, I was taken aback. I realized how much I missed the small physical gestures that communicate tenderness and consolation that is deeper than words. I found myself studying my husband's face when he wasn't looking, and noting the wrinkles and crevices that sorrow had etched; I began to consciously offer him small caresses—resting my hand on his shoulder for a minute and letting the touch linger, playfully touching the tip of his nose in a humorous moment and other loving ways known only to us."

God of the Empty Hearted and Best Kept Sacred Secrets, the energy of caring gestures, respectful touching and human intimacy between grieving people who love one another brings the most healing force there is: to feel cherished.

II

The Task Revealed

"Commit your work to the Lord, and your plans will be established. . . . How much better to get wisdom than gold! To get understanding is to be chosen rather than silver."   Proverbs 16: 3, 16

Don't look ahead and don't look behind. Stay in the work of the moment and let it carry you into the next moment.   —*Libbie Adams*

14

❧ When Grief Grows Up ❧

The child grew and became strong in spirit.   Luke 1:80

ESTRANGEMENT, alienation and dissension can be common experiences for survivors of suicide. Often wives and husbands temporarily don't have the capacity to be there for one another emotionally; children feel neglected; brothers and sisters find themselves divided. The disunity that can occur following a suicide can affect anyone, including in-laws, grandparents, cousins, aunts and uncles, friends and neighbors. Certain 'camps' or liaisons may develop as a result of disagreeing or judging why the death happened and who should have been there and wasn't. Some studies show that it is especially common for the siblings of a husband, for instance, to blame the wife for alleged shortcomings or vice versa. When this happens, (and abuse is not involved) no one wins and the trauma, grief and anguish increases for all involved—when this energy could be channeled for comfort and support.

It is also common for survivors of suicide to report feeling uncomfortable and sometimes judged when they return to work, church, school or community functions. This is how Jake explained it, "I felt as if people were whispering about me and making presumptions about my family that aren't true. It made me feel defensive and ill at ease when I was already carrying so much heartache. While mostly I experienced kindness from people, sometimes I felt unsure of who I could trust to be the kind of person who would stand by me without judging." Adolfo Quezada writes, "The ability to judge, like any God-given ability, can be used beneficially or detrimentally. It is up to us, to go beyond first impressions and opinions based on superficial information. Our judgments toward others are manifested in our treatment of them. 'You pass judgment according to appearances,' says Jesus, 'but I pass judgment on no man.' We are called to be compassionate as God is compassionate. We are to be merciful as God is merciful and not condemn others." [1]

There are also those who are forgotten or unintentionally overlooked, such as the fiancée of a young man who lost an older sister to suicide. In a support group, this sensitive young woman said tearfully, "I loved the woman who would have become my future sister-in-law too, but no one seemed to remember that. Time and time again at the funeral, people told my fiancé how sorry they were, but passed right by me on the fringes and said little or nothing. I felt neglected and not cared about. I was sad, upset, confused and since I had never experienced anything like this, I did not know how to act or what to expect. It was one of the most dreadful experiences of my whole life and I still feel a little scarred by it, even though I've basically just let it go, forgiven and moved on."

Wrestling with grudges following hurt feelings, neglect or harsh judgments by others reflects a valid response to what has been experienced. However, if these are not worked through, they will fester, poison and bring misery to the one bearing them. We can help ourselves by living the words from a reflection entitled "Do It Anyway," which have been quoted by Mother Teresa. "People are often unreasonable, illogical and self-centered; forgive them anyway. Give the world the best you have, and it may never be enough; give the world the best you've got anyway. You see, in the final analysis, it is between you and God; it was never between you and them anyway."

As Jake said, "I finally decided, out of honor to my loved one who died, that I didn't want to carry dark, vengeful or petty thoughts towards others. I wanted to carry peace in myself as much as I could so my spirit would be a clear place for my loved one's memory. This does not mean I became chummy with those who had said unfair and unkind things about me, but that I stopped obsessing about it. I no longer felt the need to explain, defend, apologize, meet their expectations or deflect ignorant, spoken and unspoken accusations regarding my character. I reaffirmed my belief in integrity, good manners, respect and tolerance. With time and persistence, I found that these things began to direct my motives, speech and actions regardless of whatever feelings I had."

God Who Bears All Our Burdens, when grief matures and grows up, we are empowered to live freely, fully and resiliently.

15

❧ Beyond the Ash Heap ❧

*Now when Job's three friends heard of all these troubles
. . . they sat with him on the ground seven days and
seven nights, and no one spoke a word to him, for they
saw his suffering was very great.*   Job 2:11a, 13

LOSING a friend to suicide can be devastating. There is a
sense of helplessness, futility, waste and even betrayal.
Marie, who lost a chronically ill friend in her thirties to suicide
wrote, "I could hardly believe this had happened. She seemed so
much better. We'd had a number of deep talks, and even though
I knew she was low, she promised me she wouldn't kill herself.
She said, "I would never do that." I sent her many emails of
encouragement and talked to her extensively on the phone. I'll
never forget her sweet voice and spirit. I had stopped worrying
about her, thought she was OK . . . and not two weeks later, her
husband contacted me to say she'd shot herself. Everyone was
completely shocked."

Sharon Allard, who has done a lot of research on this topic
offered words of sympathy and understanding, saying, "I'm sorry
about your friend. It must just tear you up. I know how much we
all want to help someone who is suicidal; while there is much we
can do, I truly believe that there comes a point in a suicidal person's life when they are so broken, so empty and in so much pain,
that they make their decision and no one can reach them. There is
an incredibly dark hole where all hope is sucked in and that

becomes their reality. Survivors of suicide need to know that a person who takes their life usually makes that decision in isolation and that decision is theirs alone. When I hear people say suicide is a totally selfish act, I know this is simply not true. The only words of comfort I can offer are that I truly believe that because of that pain, they are held so closely by God at that moment . . . who tenderly and mercifully ministers to them . . . fulfilling what we here on earth could not."

Adolfo Quezada, a therapist who works with grieving people who have lost loved ones to suicide, offered the following important words, "One mistake that is made by survivors of suicide and those who are trying to help them is that the loss is treated the same as other losses. Death by suicide is an animal all by itself. It is complicated mourning, to be sure, even different than death by homicide. It needs to be treated differently and responded to differently. One obvious mistake made by survivors of suicide is that they assume the suicide is about them (the survivors) and here is where the guilt comes in. We hear so often that suicide is preventable with appropriate and timely intervention . . . what we should be saying is that suicide is *sometimes* preventable. Other times, there is absolutely nothing that can stop someone from killing themselves. If they are stopped one day, they will succeed the next."

In an interview, he said this is what he would say to a suicide survivor regarding the myriad of feelings in the wake of such a tragedy: "It will take some time to live through this, please allow yourself that time. Suicide is such a mystery because we just don't know what is in the mind of someone who decides to take his or her own life. What is not a mystery is that your loved one was experiencing some kind of psychic pain that he/she could no longer bear. He probably believed that the pain of dying was less than the pain of living. This is what he believed at the moment of desperation. Once he decided to kill himself, there was probably a sense of peace that overtook him. Uunderstand that your loved one believed that other options were closed. This narrow thinking is part of the severe depression she was suffering from at the time. Please forgive your loved one for what happened in the midst of her illness. Forgive yourself for whatever it is that you hold against yourself about the suicide, *including having no control over it.* Commend your loved one to the Oneness of God, allow the deep grief that must take place and allow the healing to come as well. Allow a grieving God to enter the darkness with you and together shed the ocean of tears. God is with you in this dark night of mourning and God is with you in the new light of the morning. The image is one of God not so much lifting us out of our grief, but entering into it with us and staying there for as long as it takes."

God of the Ash Heap, for as long as it takes, You remind us again and again—with all our hearts, it was not our choice for our loved one to kill themselves. What we couldn't fix or control here on earth, You fix on the other side. There is no tragedy that God can't heal.

16

⟫ God's Will—A Time to Heal ⟪

...the Lord waits to be gracious to you.   Isaiah 30:18a

FOLLOWING our son's suicide, my husband, Jerry, decided to pursue a new career in the mental health field. Seeking guidance and affirmation, he was given powerful words of encouragement from a social worker who had worked passionately in that field for thirty years. She said, "I have loved my work all my life and this is the secret that has kept it rewarding: *I don't try to fix people.* What I do is support them as they learn to listen to their own hearts—where the answers and directions they seek are found."

Survivors of suicide experience profound frustration at not being able to fix the unfixable. There is a feeling of wanting to go back in time, to stay the hand, speak the words of love, comfort and support that would have changed the outcome of what happened. Sharon Allard wrote this about the illusion of affecting outcomes: "One of my most well-loved mantras is: 'I beg for surrender and all that means.' It reminds me to trust God—not to 'fix' everything, but that most of all, that God's will be done." Lily, another survivor added, "It seems clear to me, too, that if God is everywhere, then of course He is in all that happens, including tragedy. Tragedy is not His will for us, but because of free will in the world, it happens. Through faith, we learn that it is God's will to be there for us—in the hopes that we will be open, available and receptive to spiritual presence and comfort."

A grief counselor explained, "In the first year of grief, some people are not able to be comforted. They are too shell-shocked. They feel destroyed and abandoned by God. Some actually resist all attempts to comfort them. But eventually, if they keep doing the inner processing, even though they may be dragging their feet all the way, I have seen this shift occur from hopelessness to feeling good about life again. It is almost as if comfort reaches them in spite of their efforts to thwart it."

Jerry once wrote a parable about a snake named Dimitri to portray his personal grief journey: "Dimitri was lost in the Valley of Grief, traveling a treacherous, rocky path through torrential rains. Even though the night was foreboding and dark, he could sense a mountain looming in the distance. Its presence was magnetic, seeming to beckon to him. Dimitri decided he could either die on the path—alone and beaten—or press forward. Wracked with pain and grief, he summoned his strength and willpower to go on. Suddenly, something terrible happened. The ground gave way and he plunged over a cliff, hitting bottom with a crash and breaking his back. His body in ruins and unable to travel to the mountain, he listened to his beating heart.

"He began to feel ageless and a part of something larger than himself. Tears of frustration slid from his eyes because he ached for the mountain. He ached to fulfill his destiny by reaching it, but now, he knew he never would. In the blackness dwelt a presence of power, the aura of the mountain. He surrendered to it and felt happy—thinking to himself that this was death and that the mountain had come to him. But, his skin began to feel tingly and itchy. He felt as if his very molecules were shifting. He heard the words, Get up! He was suddenly filled with an uncomfortable physical need to shuffle his body. Forgetting he had a broken back, he did so. Much to his astonishment, his skin fell away. He slipped out of it like it was an old glove, where it lay shriveled and dry, a testament to old sorrows and wear and tear. It was time to move forward in a new skin, to new beginnings. His back was healed. The wind grew stronger, parting the clouds. Dimitri rose, studying the path before him bathed in light. What he saw astounded him. Rustling gently in the wind were the discarded skins of many who had passed before him. The Valley of Grief was not a place of death, but of life. In the distance, the mountain beckoned. The mountain was God."

God of New Beginnings, when we can't come to You, You come to us in ways unique and right for each of us. Comfort is Your will for us.

17

✤ Light Moments ✦

...but a broken spirit—who can bear? ...A gift opens doors; it gives access to the great." Proverbs 18:14b, 16

I WAS about to step out onto our front porch deck when a movement in the corner caught my eye. Stepping back from the sliding glass door, I peered into the growing dusk. What I saw caused me to catch my breath in shock, for there on our porch, eating nonchalantly out of our cat dish was a skunk! We have lived in our village for over two decades and I have never, in all this time, encountered a skunk in such close proximity. And even more bizarre, our black tomcat was lying nearby on a rug, completely oblivious of the skunk, as if they were friends.

Standing as still as a statue, I watched as the skunk finished eating the cat food one small morsel at a time, delicately and thoroughly cleaning up the few remaining bits that had fallen out of the dish. Not in the least bit hurried, he ambled over by the snoozing cat. Now just a yard away, I got a scrutinizing look at the small, half-grown skunk through the glass door. It was the kind known as a Striped Skunk, with glossy black fur, a snow-white double stripe on his back and a gorgeous plumed tail. I was mesmerized by his small, friendly face with a white diamond on his forehead and bright little eyes. I perceived a sense of good will about him, which I know is a very odd comment to make about a skunk.

I got on the web and searched the net for information. Are skunks the nasty creatures most people believe them to be? Are they a menace and carriers of the dreaded rabies, thereby something to be afraid of and avoided at all costs? According to research, apparently not. I learned that skunks of the striped kind are docile, non-aggressive animals who live in woodland areas and are nurturing to their young.

But, I know it is probably not a good idea to befriend a wild skunk, even though we named ours Monk and gather by the glass door every evening to watch in delight as he comes to visit just before dark. He has become familiar with our voices and recently, when I called to our cat behind our house it was not the cat who came out of the woods but Monk! Native Americans regard the skunk as powerful medicine, representing self-respect, dignity, playfulness and nonchalance in the face of mean-spiritedness or sorrow. They are also a symbol of "walking tall in spirit." It is here that our story with the little skunk deepens.

The skunk appeared around the time that our son would have graduated from high school. We were dreadfully grief-stricken and the arrival of the entertaining skunk caused a small shift for us. I found I could not help but grin through the tears and even laugh at the utter absurdity of it. If God and our son had conspired to send a funny experience to comfort, encourage and cheer us, a skunk on the doorstep of our hearts could not have been better medicine.

God Who is Master of the Ludicrous and Preposterous,
Your ingenuity in encouraging us knows no bounds.
Sometimes we forget how ingenious You can be.

18

❧ Lifter of Our Hearts ❧

For not from the east or from the west and not from the
wilderness comes lifting up; . . . But it is God . . . lifting
up another.   Psalm 75:6,7b

O NE man who lost a loved one to suicide explained, "I haven't
slept peacefully for months. I have vivid flashbacks of what
happened when something startles me and terrible nightmares.
One time, I dreamt about a wall of scissors and I woke up with
every muscle in my body tensed. I am so stricken from what happened that it is hard for me to differentiate between what is profound grief, developing anxiety disorders, panic attacks and posttraumatic stress. They all seem to overlap."

Trauma specialist Adolfo Quezada writes, "Only about a quar-
ter of those who are traumatized develop posttraumatic symptoms
in response. The more severe the trauma, the more severe the
symptoms. Where once the world was a safe and ordered place, the
posttraumatic reality is much different. Security is lost and order
turns to chaos. In the wake of traumatic events, we come to realize that it is futile to try to create absolute security for ourselves. It
is not that posttraumatic growth replaces the vulnerability that is
experienced after a traumatic event. *The paradox is that strength*
comes in and through the experience of vulnerability. The strength that
rises from the ashes of vulnerability is the strength of endurance,
acceptance, expressiveness, receptivity to help, perseverance and
the ability to overcome great odds. Our assumption that 'something like this could never happen to me' is changed forever."

Quezada explains that it is normal to feel horrified, shocked, saddened, vulnerable, outraged, and that to short circuit these emotions which need to be felt and expressed inhibits the necessary responses that lead to ultimate healing. He also says that even if a person didn't 'see' the incident or tragic event aftermath, they can well imagine it and be affected by PTSD (Post Traumatic Stress Disorder) this way. "Those who experience intrusive thoughts or flashbacks of the traumatic experience have nightmares and suffer from hyperarousal or extreme startle response to unexpected noises or movements. The healing process gets underway for trauma survivors when they begin to free themselves from being victims of the trauma. As the trauma survivors regain more and more control over aspects of their life, they begin to overcome the effects of trauma. This sense of freedom makes all the difference in the world."

This reality is profoundly illustrated in the journey of Sandy, a beautiful young girl who was our son's girlfriend and whom we remain very close to. On the first year anniversary of his death, she wrote, "It has been a very hard year. I was trying to forgive my boyfriend, cope with the pain, help others and simply just get on with my life. At first, I was really scared to get close to anyone because I didn't want to lose them or feel betrayed again. But I realized if you never take chances, you can't even live life. For awhile, I was afraid of forgetting my boyfriend, but now I know he'll always be a part of me. I've hurt so much this year and in so many ways, but I think all this made me a much stronger person. It really made me realize how much everyone means to me and to never take anything or anyone for granted." As Sandy's grief transformed from pain over a traumatic loss to 'love remembered,' she wrote a goodbye letter to our son on the first anniversary of his death, saying, "I still have some hard times, but I'm doing better.

One day we'll meet again and you can answer all my questions. You were my first love and I'll never forget you. I'm going to live my life to the fullest like I know you would want me to. I'm moving on and I'm happy and I know you're happy for me, too. I love you with my whole heart and rest in peace."

Writing this letter brought some closure for Sandy, illustrating, as Quezada writes, ". . . life suddenly seems more precious than before. In the aftermath, there seems to be more closeness among family and friends and more intimacy in significant relationships. Part of this stems from a renewed willingness to be more self-disclosing with thoughts and feelings. Affection is expressed more openly and communication is authentic. People say that their beliefs have gotten stronger and that in general, persons get more in touch with the spiritual elements of their life after a traumatic event . . . we are witnessing the resilience of the human spirit and its capacity to rebound and continue to grow, *not in spite of the trauma but through and because of it.*" As another survivor of suicide aptly described this phenomenon, "following the second year of my grief, I felt as if I were rising out of a coma . . . awakening to a spiritual buoyancy that while subtle, lifted my whole outlook on life and death."

Divine Lifter of our Hearts, when we can't help ourselves and relive horrific memories over and over, You gently remind us: the traumatic events that led to our loved one's death happened only once; they did not die over and over . . . they live now forever, in peace and eternal life—as will we, one day.

19

❧ God Applauds Self Care ☙

A new heart I will give you, and a new spirit I will put within you.   Ezekiel 36:26

THE grief of losing a loved one to suicide can, like any grief, affect a person's physical well-being. People forget to take care of themselves, exercise or be mindful of nutrition, which if gone unchecked, can lead to unhealthy results. Thomas Moore, in his book, *Care of the Soul,* describes self care like this: "Care of the soul is not a project of self-improvement nor a way of being released from the troubles and pains of human existence. We care for the soul solely by honoring its expressions, by giving it time and opportunity to reveal itself and by living life in a way that fosters the depth, interiority and the quality in which it flourishes." [2] Through these words, we are compelled to remember that taking care of ourselves is not purely an emotional activity but a physical one as well—as we learn to seek wellness of body, mind and soul.

Jill, an office manager explained, "I gradually put on weight without taking note of it. I knew I was eating to fill the emptiness, but I was processing so many things, it was the last thing for me to address, the one thing I always put off. It really hit home when I went to my doctor who said in no uncertain terms that I needed to lose weight or I could develop diabetes, which my blood tests revealed were borderline." Even then, Jill said that acknowledging she had gotten so overweight was not enough to motivate her to change. Time slid by and she put on even more weight. "I've always been so disciplined in my work," she said, "even meticulous, which gave me a sense of satisfaction but the discipline needed to control my weight was always an issue." For most survivors of suicide, the lifestyle elements that were challenging when life was normal tend to become much more complex and pronounced for a time. Understanding the educational dynamics of this can go a long way in keeping them in check and under control, whether it be addictions to smoking, alcohol, sports, relentless activity, workaholism or any number of things.

Jill said, "Guilt began to needle me that I was not monitoring what I ate and as my grief progressed, I was eventually able to take an honest look at the weight gain and why I had this problem. I think I may have been more discouraged than I realized, which played a factor in my inability to change. I had also grown bored and was eating to fill boredom, find comfort and relieve stress. One day, I did something very smart that made me very proud of myself." Jill says she created an alcove just for her, with her treadmill as the focal point. She began by making a commitment to being faithful to using it each day. On a shelf above her treadmill, she placed a photo of her loved one, a meditation candle, meaningful objects, a small book which listed people she wanted to pray for, bottled water, vitamins and calcium tablets, a 'slim' photo of herself for inspiration and a poem about not spiritually waiting for others to 'bring flowers to you, but planting your own garden.' She also put a scale by her treadmill, a full-length mirror, and for incentive, displayed an outfit which she realistically felt she could lose enough weight to wear again. She called this new experiment her *'appointment with herself,'* a new beginning that ushered in a new habit with a new routine. She also included music, which she alternated between rock and roll Golden Oldies and softer, more reflective music, depending on what her mood needed at the time. The very act of creating this space energized her. She also wrote to several friends about this change she wanted to make in her life as a way of affirming her new intentions.

In *The Artist's Way*, Julia Cameron teaches that "enthusiasm is not an emotional state. It is a spiritual commitment, a loving surrender to our creative process, a loving recognition of all the creativity around us." [3] Through Jill's enthusiastic story, Cameron's words remind us of the intricate and important interconnectedness of grief, emotional soul work and physical well-being.

God Who Calls Us to be Caretakers of Ourselves, thank You for Your spiritual ovation; sometimes we don't realize that feeling good about ourselves again is one of the greatest gifts we can give not only ourselves, but our loved one who died.

20

❧ A Living Compass ❧

Thanks be to God for his indescribable gift!
2 Corinthians 9:15

HOLIDAYS are especially tough for survivors of suicide. The emptiness and 'presence of absence' of the missing loved one is never more apparent, painful or poignant. As one survivor said, "You get used to it . . ." but happiness is never the same. There is an important lesson to be learned here; as Adolfo Quezada explains in his new book *Rising From the Ashes,* "being happy is not the same as being joyful. Joy is a consequence of our faith, joy emanates from God . . . happiness comes and goes with the wind of circumstance." [4] For the bereaved, that promise of faith and joy often brings memories and symbols that give one courage, direction and the comfort needed to go on. This happened for me, as I faced the third Christmas without our son. I wrote:

"Dusk has fallen, but it is so white and luminous from the snow-storm you can still see uptown in our village from the porch. The air seems foggy or like it is filled with static electricity, the sound reminiscent of a deep, faraway ocean roaring in the woods. The creaking tree trunks appear coal black in contrast to the whiteness, their armpits and undersides flocked from storm-driven snow. Like black and white winter garter snakes, the corkscrew willow branches entwine and coil in the wind.

"The snow has drifted across the yards, houses, stalled cars and thorny shrubbery, blurring boundaries while the heavily-laden branches of the giant evergreen trees droop with the weight. Their limbs seem alive in the storm, lifting here and there and seeming to whisper a language that only the wild creatures know. The street lights blink on, one by one, glowing dully like hazy bronze-colored portals or beacons into another world. And thus it comes, the arrival of our first snowstorm of the year—beautiful beyond words—and sometimes fierce, like life.

"Closing the door on the scene and gathering the neck of my cardigan tighter, I stand warming my outstretched hands before our fireplace. Well acquainted with portals of the heart, I slip easily into another time and place: It is a perfect night, our village streets deserted, the breeze faint and cool. Mic and I are taking a midnight bike ride, our traditional farewell to summer. The moon dominates, casting white patches on the road through the leafy branches. Grinning, Mic describes it perfectly as a giant flashlight in the sky. Our bike tires crunch loudly on the loose gravel and the sound seems intrusive in the otherwise absence of sound. 'Shhh,' we say, as we pass the darkened houses. It seems we're the only ones awake.

"We pedal slowly, breathing deeply and not talking. The corn-field looms dark and dense, a presence in the night you can feel. Suddenly, our tires hit the main street pavement and we glide along silently now, in sync with the night energy. All the while, we keep our faces upturned toward the moon, which like a compass, seems to guide us. There is not a dog or cat in sight and not even any frogs croaking. We bike to our destination—the stop sign bordering the highway—and turning around, coast back down to the pop machine. Four quarters later find Mic and I perching companionably on the picnic table in the gazebo nestled in the park—sentries giving witness to the change of seasons."

The memory fades and I return to the present, a sentry now to the coming of the third Christmas following the death of our son. My heart has become a living compass that guides me to beacons of faith that comfort. Along with many others, I give witness to the endurance and resilience of the human spirit. And while the wise men followed a star to Bethlehem, in my mind I envision the star as a giant flashlight that shines through eternal portals of love.

Christmas God of Gifts of the Heart, to become a living compass is the most profound gift that happens to us . . . completely and utterly beyond words.

21

✣ Names of God ✣

. . . those who know your name put their trust in you.

Psalm 9:10

IN his book, *Prayers for a Planetary Pilgrim,* Edward Hays
writes what he calls a Psalm to Virgin Spring. When I was 49,
I understood more fully than I ever had in my life what that
means. I had written, "This spring feels like a first time, never-
before-seen spring to me. I marvel at the unexpected anticipa-
tion I am feeling. I never thought I could bear spring again."
When our son died a year before, I had named that first spring
Black Spring. The first tulip, the first warm breeze, the first call
of the wild geese all reminded me that even though the earth
was being reborn, our son was not a part of it and nothing would
ever bring him back. Later, in looking back at my image journal
I drew at that time, I was surprised to see that I entitled the page
"Dead-Head Woman: Rebirth of Feelings." Beneath a sketch of
a woman I had drawn shrouded in black, holding a single shoot
of green grass, I wrote of my rebellion of spring, "How dare it
come?" Yet, I concluded the page with the words, *"I am being
won over . . . not to joy . . . but to something secret, growing and green
within me that I can't name."*

Looking back, I know that I was experiencing the first comforting blade of Divine Consolation. Ed Hays writes in a prayer, "O
you who are beyond all names, yet whom we call Father and
Mother . . . unfold for me your best kept secret . . ." Throughout his

book he "names" God as revelations come to him. Some of these include: Never-Tiring Miracle Worker, Radiant Rain God, Timeless and Ever-Youthful God, Wind of Inspiration, Loving Source of Sacred Cycles, Life Force of the Rising and Setting Sun, Holy Womb of Life and Ever-New One." [5] These life-affirming names of God spoke to me and reminded me of the vastness of God.

Naming God as we discover who God is, is a sacred act of the soul. There is an intimacy in the names God discloses or confides to each of us in our hearts as we journey through life. In my previously published books, I suddenly realized that I had listed over eighty of my own names of who God is to me personally. All of these names were wrought out of life experiences that were very personal to me. Some included: God of Lanterns Within Our Breasts, God Who Mothers Starving Souls, Hovering-Ever Present Mother God, God of Empty Nests and Loved Ones Who Have Crossed Over, Sweeping-Swooshing God Who Knows No Boundaries, God of Flowers That Bloom in the Night and Tender-Hearted God of Fallen Trees and Bare-Branched People, to name only a few.

As I named God "Hope of Virgin Spring," I thought of what Judith Duerk wrote in *Circle of Stones, Woman's Journey to Herself,* "How might your life have been different if there had been a place . . . a place where, after the fires were lighted, and the drumming, and the silence, you would claim, finally, in your Naming, as you spoke slowly into that silence, that the time had come, full circle, for you also to reach out . . ." [6]

I asked myself what would be a name for God that encompassed all others—that embraced God as our father and our mother, our sister and our brother, beyond gender, time and space? For me, the answer came in an eureka moment, when I read a column by Thomas C. Fox, who also was wondering the same thing. During an enlightening trip to India, his friend Saldanha provided the profound, simple but deep answer: *God is your Best Friend.* [7] Looking back, I think that name was the secret, green, unnamed thing that was growing in me, reaching out as it does to all of us . . . beyond those seasons when spring in our hearts feels black.

God Whose Names Number like Grains of Sand in the Sea, when You name Yourself to each of us privately and intimately in our hearts, You are telling us that no one can take our place in Your life—that without us in Your heart, there would be a nameless hole.

22

✤ A Million Brushing Wings ✤
Letting Go

And I say, O that I had wings . . . I would fly away and
be at rest.   Psalm 55:6

BEGINNING to let go of the grief is one of the most wrenching aspects survivors of suicide face. We mistakenly think that if we let go of the terrible sorrow we are also letting go of our loved one who has died. We long to cling to their memory as if that would somehow keep them close to us and enable us to hold on to them. We do not always understand that how long we grieve is not an indication of how much we loved the person. There comes a point when continuing on with wrenching tears and agonizing over what happened is not good for us.

My husband and I often drive along the Minnesota River bottom where winding, narrow gravel roads take us through beautiful woodlands. That first stunning autumn following our son's death, we took these drives often to seek comfort in nature. My grief at this point was all-consuming and frantic as if I were running inconsolably down long, unending hallways within myself. I needed to begin making a transition, but I didn't know how or what it even was. It was at this point that I had an extraordinary experience that I never forgot.

As we were driving, we came to a unique place where the trees bend over the road like a canopy, creating a hollow. Within this vaulted arch thousands of migrating orange and black monarch butterflies had gathered. They filled the trees, the sky and the air. Spellbound, we stopped to watch the phenomenal sight. I literally felt that if I stepped out of the car, I could spread my arms and they could gather me up as into a winged apron for safe-keeping and carry me away. The whole world for that brief moment in time seemed to stand still. It was as if a sacred hush had fallen as silent and golden as a prayer. The serenity of all those thousands of silent, fanning wings somehow momentarily quieted my aching heart.

I've always looked back on that experience as the threshold day that God reached out to me and asked me to begin letting go of my grief for my own sake—to let love gather me up—and to understand that my son did not want me to suffer so. It's not something you can understand until it happens to you, but there comes a point in time when we each are gently asked to let go. The experience I had reminds me of the poem that accompanies Mary Southard's painting, "Woman's Song of Peace":

> The song of peace is woman's song.
> She sings the song of life's seasons—
> rhythms of birth and death, receiving and giving,
> times of waiting and fulfillment, suffering and joy.
> She sings a gentle song of listening and hope,
> of wholeness and unity,
> of harmony with earth
> and reverence for earth's gifts.
> Her song is compassion,
> her song is love.
> If nations would be healed,
> woman's song must be sung.
> If there would be peace,
> woman's song must be heard.

God of a Million Brushing Wings, when our hearts are heavy, You call us to freedom that only flight of the spirit can bring.

23

ꙮ Map of the Heart ꙮ

. . .but your eyes shall see your Teacher. And when you turn to the right or when you turn to the left, your ears shall hear a word behind you saying, "This the way; walk in it."   Isaiah 30:20b, 21

MANY people who are processing the tragedy of losing a loved one to suicide find that creating a visual journal as a place to vent and discover insights can be a marvelous coping tool. I called mine *Joni's Map of the Heart.* In it, I drew over forty-five images, phrases and affirmation statements, all in crayon in a large sketch book, covering a time period of about a year. Through my image journal, not only could I initially express my feelings, but later, use it to remind myself of important heart revelations that I never wanted to forget as I sought to find my way. On days of doubt, I could look at it and feel encouraged by the healing progress I was making.

Creating a visual journal is easy. The only requirement is making a decision and commitment to begin. On my first page, in bold slashing colors of red and black, I drew what I called "The Scream," which was an open mouth with the word *why* zigzagged through it representing a rent in the universe. The accompanying phrase read, "The day the earth stood still." This early image was followed by a sketch of a woman bent over, dragging a ball and chain. I called her Weight of the World Woman, shackled to feelings of despair.

By the third image, I was already instinctively seeking hope, drawing a white flag representing a pure heart, with the word *truth* written on it to remind me that the callous untruths of a few who were judging our situation did not change the real truth that love knows and that I know. There was an image of the sun setting forever on life as we knew it and a sketch of a woman washed up on an ocean beach. Beneath this was the phrase written in the sand, "Friends are a Nation" by Emily Dickinson to represent the support of friends and family who rallied around us and especially my sisters who were a constant source of practical help and comfort. There was a drawing of a box with the lid off, with the words, "God is out of the box and will never return," followed by a woman named Surrender. She stood with empty hands raised in prayer, echoing the words of Mary, "Let it be done to me as you say."

By the eleventh image, comfort was finding me in bits and pieces, represented by the image of a woman cradled in a hand that reached out of a cosmic swirl, with the phrase, "God is not only above, within and all around, but I am within God." On the next page, I drew a picture of a woman being rescued and pulled out of a pit by a rope attached to a glittering star, with the caption, "Passion draws and pulls us to our highest calling, it does not push." Next, on what would have been our son's eighteenth birthday, I drew an image of a sacred egg being released into a stream of love, with the words, "Letting go brings love back to us."

There were many images to follow such as a life preserver, an image of a spread-out deck of cards, with the slogan, "Put your voice out there, let the cards fall where they may," when I was feeling worried about having my work approved by others. Next came an image of a pregnant woman, with the beautiful words, "I am pregnant with myself, we hold the future here in our wombs,"[8] taken from the book *Stars in Your Bones* by Alla Bozarth, Julia Barkley and Terri Hawthorne. By image number twenty-six, I was discovering the clarity of knowing what my needs were, as I drew an image of a spiritual midwife, called a *Doula,* which is a Greek word for labor assist when a woman is giving birth. The phrase below it was, "I believe that for grief to give birth to peace, there must be the support and care of others who also give you the space you need."

Other images were those of a monster in jail, representing the confining and setting aside of negative thoughts, such as, "You don't deserve to be happy." There was Boundary Woman, whose very body was a map, followed by a drawing of a suitcase, with a quote from John Steinbeck in *Travels With Charley,* "We do not take a trip, the trip takes us." [9] I drew a playground teeter-tooter, with weighted boxes balancing each side, stating, "Desperation is giving rise to ease." There was an image of a childhood hay mow, with rays of light streaming down from the barn cupola, where you could see dust particles floating in the beams of light, like microscopic souls, with the slogan, "We are all interconnected, how we choose to live affects the whole." Finally, on the last page, I drew a giant, double rainbow, as seen by my middle son and his lovely wife. The conclusion statement read: "The rainbow is a sign of blessing and covenant. It promises joy, completion and new hope." With that, as I prayerfully tucked my journal away, I celebrated my ongoing survival of the heart. Following that first year of loss, it was like a miracle to me.

God of the Terrorized, when we stand stranded by the roadside of our shattered hearts, You promise, "I will show you the way."

24

❧ Floodlights of Love ❧

*I will leave none of them behind; and I will never again
hide my face from them, when I pour out my spirit upon
the house of Israel, says the Lord God.*

Ezekiel 39:28b, 29

JOHN is one of my closest friends. He has a master's degree
in Industrial Relations, has worked as a Human Resources
director in the healthcare industry for the last two decades and
is one of the most amazing people I've ever met. He is a professional singer who has performed at Carnegie Hall, exquisite
humorist . . . and he is gay. When I asked him what he would be
able to offer to survivors of suicide who have lost a loved one
who is gay, he sent me excerpts from his life story. He knows
what he's talking about, because twenty-two years ago, he himself tried to commit suicide.

The first thing he sent me were statistics: "Studies on youth suicide consistently find that lesbian and gay youth are 2-6 times
more likely to attempt suicide than any other youth and may
account for 30% of all completed suicides among teens." [10] In a
Massachusetts study, 46% who identify as gay, lesbian or bisexual
had attempted suicide in the past year compared to 8.8 of their
peers, and 23.5% required medical attention as a result of a suicide attempt compared to 3.3% of their peers." [11] He also sent one
of his favorite quotes by Ralph Waldo Emerson, which John writes,
says it all: *"To laugh often and much, to win the respect of intelligent*

people and the affection of children; to earn the appreciation of honest
critics and endure the betrayal of false friends; to appreciate beauty; to
find the best in others; to leave the world a bit better, whether by a healthy
child, a garden patch, or a redeemed social condition; to know even one
has breathed easier because you have lived. This is to have succeeded."

With this as a foreword, John then writes, "I tried to kill myself
when I was eighteen. The reason: I had come to the conclusion
that my sexuality, which seemed undeniably different from everyone else, could not and would not be accepted or tolerated by the
world I knew. So, one night, just past midnight, I swallowed half a
bottle of aspirin and a dozen tranquilizers. I undressed, placed my
neatly folded clothes on a chair, and went to bed, terrified but certain I was doing the right thing for everyone. However, as I lay
there, feeling increasingly drowsy, nauseous and—I don't know,
wild and crazy—I jolted upright in my bed at the realization that
This Was It. No more me. No more life. No more anything. I
dragged Mom from a sound sleep, confessed what I had done and
began sobbing. Shaken, but now completely awake, she forced per-
oxide down my throat and I survived. My father, a career alcoholic,
coldly said, "If the boy wants to kill himself, I won't stand in his
way."

John says that this experience, along with many others was like
a floodlight on a prisoner trying to escape. He realized he could
run but could not hide forever. Thus began his passage to self-
knowledge, mental stability, self-confidence and well-being.
Having been in a committed relationship for thirteen years, John
writes, "I wouldn't change who I am for anything. This is me. This
is who I am." He has kept vigil with people dying of AIDS and he
understands the sorrow of losing loved ones to suicide only too
well, having lost a number of friends that way. More than anything,

John counsels those who are mourning not to blame themselves, to keep the loved one's memory alive and to live the words offered by Emerson in memory of the one who died. "Remember that the torment your loved one knew that caused them to take their life is gone," John says. "They are at peace and they want you to be, too. Cherish the good times; embrace the bad experiences your loved one knew; learn from them but then let them go. Allow your grief to be transformed into a motivating force that can change the world into a better place that calls for inclusion, dignity and diversity. Let this be your loved one's legacy."

God Who Floodlights the Human Heart with Unconditional Love, we are all, each and every one of us, created in your divine image. Grief and the power of divine consolation know no bounds regardless of race, color, creed or sexual orientation.

25

❧ The Lighthouse—Beacon of Faith ☙

Indeed, you are my lamp, O Lord, the Lord lightens my
darkness.   2 Samuel 22:29

SYMBOLS can offer powerful images of hope and strength
and the lighthouse is undoubtedly one of the most provoca-
tive and seems to speak to the human heart with a language all
its own. Libbie Adams, who lives in close proximity to an old
lighthouse, writes beautifully of the alluring landscape, "Windswept and isolated, the tiny island of Core Banks rests among
the treacherous shoals of the Atlantic Ocean on the Outer Banks
of North Carolina. Its only permanent inhabitants are the
wildlife that make the island home. Raucous seagulls soar in on
the updrafts from the ocean, spreading their wings above the
lapping waters, sending the crabs dashing for safety in the surf.
Everywhere, strewn upon the beaches, are extraordinary conch
shells that have been tossed upon the shore by rolling waves that
ebb and tide. And in their retreat from the shore, the waves continually flush away the telltale signs of the wild mustangs that for
centuries have roamed among the sea oats and sand dunes, following in the footsteps of their fathers."

"Yet is the lighthouse, the ever-faithful lighthouse, towering over
all else, that is the indisputable captain of the shoals," Libbie
explains. "Its massive structure rises one hundred and sixty nine
feet above the Atlantic, sending its beacon of safety and direction
to all who look to it for guidance. It is sure and dependable, never
slumbering. What a strong and comforting presence in the midst

of danger! And what an awesome example for the human spirit to follow."

Years ago, when my friend, Gary Frye and I facilitated a web site for the chronically ill, Gary named our site "The Lighthouse Café." I asked Gary why the image of a lighthouse meant so much to him and this is what he said: "The image of light and the safety a lighthouse projects has always had a calming effect on me. I am fascinated by the fact that a lighthouse can project such a penetrating beacon of light while in reality, its actual light source is really quite modest. The early lighthouse source of light was a simple, small oil lamp. Today, lighthouses are powered by electricity but the light itself is still relatively small and depends on magnification and direction. How can such a small light be directed and magnified in order for it to be seen through fog and storms? This is accomplished by the use of a *Fresnel lens*. A Fresnel lens is thick polished glass that is cut at intricate angles, which actually bend and direct the light source. Thinking about a Fresnel lens brings me vivid images that I can relate to with regard to our spirit. Do we have a Fresnel spirit? I think we do."

Gary continues, "Everything in our life can affect the light and spirit that we project. This includes the sickness, the hurt, mistakes and all of the burdens that we carry within us. Every human being walking this earth is a potential lighthouse. We all have a light within us; our light is surrounded by God's spirit, which I relate to as our Fresnel lens. Our Fresnel lens is there to magnify and guide this light. Just as a lighthouse keeper must maintain the physical part of a Fresnel lens by keeping it clean and clear of anything that might limit the effectiveness of the light, we must be aware of all those things that can prohibit our inner light. In order to address all the obstacles that become burdens and therefore cause our light to become dim, we must take advantage of the serenity that dwells within us. As the well-known Serenity Prayer advises, "God, grant me the serenity to accept the things I cannot change, the courage to change the things I can, and the wisdom to know the difference."

Gary's merging of the lighthouse image, Fresnel lens and Serenity Prayer offers important insights to those whose lives have been shattered by the suicide of a loved one. In response, I wrote, "Light is traditionally associated with spirit or God, a sign of spiritual life within; the lighthouse image reminds us that when we feel as if we are plunged into darkness, God is a beacon to us. When we feel as if we are drowning and storm-tossed, the symbolism of God as a lighthouse offers a perspective that is powerful and easy to grasp. In responding to the image, we discover that we always have God to turn to and that no situation or feeling is hopelessly beyond spiritual consolation. When our strength is temporarily gone and we are consumed and battered with doubt, the image of the lighthouse promises that God's light, love and faithfulness to us will guide us to healing harbors where we will feel safe again and sure of ourselves. We will be all right, because nothing can take the light of God in our hearts away from us. It is an eternal light that warms us from the inside out. It is the light of comfort.

God whose Guiding Beacon of Light Dwells Eternally Within, You penetrate our darkest despair and magnify the tiniest ray of hope within us. Within the waves of our grief and tears, You remind us that serenity is possible through the lens of faith.

26

❧ God of the Impossible ☙

*They were greatly astounded and said to one another,
"Then who can be saved?" Jesus looked at them and
said, "For mortals it is impossible, but not for God; For
God, all things are possible."*   Mark 10:26, 27

IN her groundbreaking book, *Lights in the Darkness: For
Survivors and Healers of Sexual Abuse,* Sister Ave Clark, O.P.
writes, speaking for those who have been sexually abused or who
have lost a loved one to suicide because of it, "We need to give
support to others who battle the collapse of their spirits and lift
them up so they will not be among the 1.5% of deaths listed as
suicide." Sister Ave, who herself was abused and who has created a compassionate retreat ministry, Heart to Heart, has also
lost beloved friends to suicide. Deeply understanding the pain
from both sides, she says, "Survivors of suicide and survivors of
abuse have to walk in and out of tragedy and somehow not let it
ruin the rest of their lives. We can choose; we can decide to heal,
to celebrate and to embrace the suffering and find meaningful
ways to live with hope for ourselves and others. We can learn
very slowly to let go and let God guide us with companions who
remain steadfast and help us to reclaim, rebuild and rediscover
love in the ruins." [12]

The following courageous woman, Sarah, a medical professional, offers insights that could only be shared by someone who
has been there. She writes, "I'm certain that sexual abuse does
indeed account for many attempts. As a survivor of several dif-

ferent forms of abuse, I have found the pain, scars, the feelings of shame and degradation of the sexual abuse I endured deeply intense and difficult to deal with. I understand the value of education that teaches that most suicides result from undiagnosed, untreated and unrecognized depression, however I feel that statement alone sounds superficial. In my experience, people are depressed by a great many things and often with good and valid reasons. Yet, the majority of those afflicted do not take their own lives. In order to survive sexual abuse, the victim often creates a completely new and imagined reality which can be as simple as just pretending that the abuse is not happening, to the extreme of developing multiple personalities to cope with the trauma. The official term for multiplicity is Dissociative Disorder."

The general public would be shocked, Sarah explains, if they knew how many people in this country have been or are being abused. Telling the truth about this far-reaching epidemic, Sarah pointedly reveals why some do go on to kill themselves. She teaches, "The all-pervasive sense of guilt and shame, the inability to see that the abuse was not something they had any control over, the constant feeling that no one really knows who they are, the severe sense of isolation, the sense of contamination to the core and the perceived certainty that it will never go away, the belief that nothing we do will ever be 'good enough' to justify taking up space and using up resources in the world despite evidence to the contrary, even the possibility of being programmed by cruel and profoundly sick perpetrators to believe that you must kill yourself before you 'tell the secrets,' all leave permanent scars."

Sarah has written many powerful, assertive journals and through her writing, ministers to others. She speaks of being overwhelmed with the knowledge of how gifted she is in this life, referring to heart knowledge, clarity, joy, and the pleasure of 'being' as treasures waiting for everyone, no matter what their life circumstances. These excerpts from some of her many works, like Sister Ave Clark's writings, speak to both those who have survived abuse and those who are mourning the suicide of a loved one who was abused. Sarah writes, "For each of us, the shadows are different; they are our own private specters and ghosts and must be confronted in our own way, in our own time; but the message is always constant and unmutable. We must live for who we are today and stay in the present moment. We must honor and then free our ghosts of the past, we must continue the unending journey into the light of God's ever-calling love."

Concluding with prophetic verse, Sarah presents a message that she feels God would say: "Take care of your soul, your very core wherein I dwell. Remember that you can change no one but yourself and then only when you are open to my grace. Let your life be an example of how one life lived truly and fully can be an encouragement and inspiration to another. Let me live in you and transform your pain; let me live in you and feel joy. Live in me and be all that I call you to be. Listen to my voice and look for my face wherever you are. I am here . . . *Abba*"

God Who Empowers the Powerless, when the worst has happened, Your spirit envisions us as brave of heart, tall in spirit and spiritually whole in mind, body and soul. When we can't believe it will happen, You believe for us, reminding us that with You, all things are possible.

III

A New Identity

From now on, therefore, we regard no one from a human point of view; even though we once knew Christ from a human point of view, we know him no longer in that way. So if anyone is in Christ, there is a new creation: everything old has passed away; see, everything has become new! All this is from God . . .

2 Corinthians 5:16, 17, 18a.

Just as a garden needs time to lie fallow, so too do our places that give life to our creativity. Take time to nurture your spirit with rest and allow new life to take over in the ground you have so diligently tilled, turned and tended. Honor your fallowness, for it is in quietness that new thoughts, ideas and insights are nurtured and grow, so that you can bring them to fruition when you are ready.

—Sharon Allard

27

✥ An Empty Nest and Beyond ✥

*Neither death, nor life, nor angels, nor rulers, nor things
present, nor things to come, nor powers, nor height, nor
depth nor anything else in all creation, will be able to sep-
arate us from the love of God . . .*   Romans 8:38-39

WHEN we begin letting go of our grief, the one thing we
need is assurance that by doing so, we are not going to be
left with a void of nothing. We need to know with certainty that our
hearts will not be left empty. One day, I had an experience that
helped me understand why letting go is necessary. A friend had
sent me a magazine clipping of a pair of hands cradling an empty
nest and reaching toward heaven. Above the nest, being drawn
toward a sacred realm of light, was an egg. The image evoked a
powerful sense of connection for me.

Just weeks prior to our son's death, I had started work on my
second book. Since I anticipated that my writing would involve a
great deal of inner work and personal incubation, I had placed an
egg by my computer—a powerful symbol of new life and, for me,
a symbol of this new phase of my journey. In many ancient tradi-
tions, in fact, the egg represents immortality. At the time, of course,
I had no way of knowing what that small egg would come to mean
to me. Following our son's death, I often thought about dashing
out into the woods and smashing the egg against a tree as an
expression of my grief and desperation. Somehow, though, I just
couldn't bring myself to do that.

After four months, however, my egg began to spoil, and I finally knew what I had to do. I carefully placed the spoiling egg in a tiny brass pail and headed for the woods, following a familiar trail to a place where a creek splashes across a rock-strewn stream bed just below a beaver dam. This has always been a sacred prayer place for me, overshadowed by what I call The Great Grandmother Trees.

Standing there, I prayed that God would comfort my family, our son's friends and me in our grief. Speaking at length about the sorrow, the despair, the horror, the wonder of our lives, the mystery and hope of feeling our son was "gone but not truly gone," I clutched to my breast the small pail holding the decaying egg. As I prayed, a giant great horned owl flew silently into view and landed on a large branch of a Great Grandmother Tree, seeming to keep vigil just above me. I could see his round, wide eyes which seemed both solemn and benevolent.

As the owl watched, I slipped the egg out of the pail and let it slide into the still water at my feet. Lingering for only a moment, it slowly began to tumble into the middle of the stream, pulled along by the gentle current. I watched, feeling it was important to witness this journey. Then, a surprising thing happened. For no apparent reason, the egg drifted back toward me and came to rest, again, at my feet. It occurred to me in that moment that *letting go brings love back to us* in different and powerful dimensions we really can't comprehend. With tears stinging my eyes, I watched the egg rest briefly at my feet and then float back again into the middle of the creek where it resumed its slow journey downstream. As I glanced up, the owl lifted silently, his monstrous wings sweeping him from sight.

Night had begun to fall and I could barely see as I made my way back through the woods. It seemed to me as if God had sent the owl to keep vigil, thereby assuring me that I was doing the right thing in releasing my son, my sorrow, my dreams and hopes, allowing the stream of life and God's care to surround, enfold and carry us all. The egg seemed so small and fragile in the stream. I felt very protective of it—but I sensed that it was time to trust, to symbolically let it go on to wherever it was meant to go.

In the near darkness, the branches of the winter trees were silhouetted against the sky, and I could see the many empty nests the trees lifted heavenward, as if in supplication, like prayers. Reminded of the magazine clipping that my friend had sent me, I felt somehow comforted. Clutching the now empty brass pail to my breast, as I had earlier, I thought of "emptiness," of an empty cocoon, of Christ's tomb—and then I thought of resurrection. As gratitude for hope filled me, I knew I would find the courage to go on.

God of Empty Nests and Loved Ones Who Have Crossed Over, there is an invisible realm of spirit that weaves itself into and beyond the world we see with only the human eye. When it is time to let go of our grief, the love which was always there begins to flow freely again.

28

❧ They Dwelt Among Us ❧
and Still Do

How lovely is your dwelling place, O Lord of hosts! My soul longs, indeed it faints for the courts of the Lord; . . . Happy are those who live in your house.

Psalm 84:1,2a,4a

THE sacred space we create in our homes can be an act of the soul. Through the intimate design and use of color, pattern, balance, texture, sacred objects and the play of light and shadow, we can create a haven for our grief to dwell, an atmosphere that is receptive to tears, hope and healing. When our son died, our home became such a great comfort to us that I decided to write its story:

"It was 1974 and love at first sight. My husband and I, newly married, waded through the waist high grass to get to the front double doors of the old, empty church. Mounting the large cement steps with banisters on each side and heaving the heavy doors open, we stepped into the vestibule, which led to another set of wooden swinging doors. Dusty sunlight filtered in from the arched glass window high above the door and the place was silent and peaceful as a tomb. Walking into the main part of the church, cluttered with magazines, debris, old furniture and a bed, we noted the gorgeous, tin-sculpted ceiling and hanging white-globe light fixtures with holes in them from being shot out by vandals, like most of the eight large, cathedral windows. As we approached the altar at the north end of the building, our tennis shoes crept soundlessly on the friendly, pine boards of the floor throughout.

"Holding hands and descending stairs to the church basement which had seen many church dinners, we found more debris, leaves, dead animals and darkness. I shuddered a bit at that, but as we slipped outside and sat on the steps and gazed at the southern blue sky and the village main street just a block away, a dream was born in me. A dream to own the old church and make it our home. Before long, we were able to purchase it for a song and the work began. Oh, how we underestimated the work it would take to transform the old church into a home!

"Over thirty years later, it seems a wonder to my husband and I that the years have passed as quickly as they have. Our house, which we named Annie, now has black and rose Victorian carpet throughout, and flooded with the amber light from the three large restored cathedral windows, has sheltered our hopes, dreams and joys as we raised our three sons. Before we bought our home, it was steeped in prayers of every kind as its congregation held funerals, weddings, baptisms and services of every kind. Now, Annie is steeped in our family's love, grief, memories and nurturing care.

It has been a journey of transformation as we designed and remodeled Annie's space year after year—all the while, experiencing the same process within our own hearts as we found our way again and began adjusting to life without our Mic. We learned to allow our sorrow to teach us things, enlarge our hearts and enhance our way of looking at the world. More than ever, we realize that a house can be a world within a world, where the people who live there can find serenity, beauty and consolation. This was never more apparent to us than when we lost our son. His picture now hangs in a small alcove and we light a candle under it whenever we are lonely for him. His laughter filled this house for seventeen years and it remains in the ongoing love we have for him."

God Who Makes Your Dwelling in Human Hearts, we often forget that the living energy of love permeates the spaces in which we live . . . so much so, that we are drenched in it and don't even realize it.

29

❧ The Great Continuance ❧

He has sent me to bring good news to the oppressed, to bind up the brokenhearted, to comfort all who mourn; ... They shall build up the ancient ruins, they shall raise up the former devastations; they shall repair the ruined cities.   Isaiah 61:1b,2b, 4

ABOUT six months following our son's death, I began to have renovation dreams. While still grief-stricken and not consciously aware of any inner spiritual shifts, four dreams I had began to portray a very different story. I dreamt that our former pastor who had died years ago was overseeing the building of a new church. This new church was acres big, with only the newly-poured cement foundation laid. It was astonishing because this was no ordinary, earthly cement. When you walked on it, it felt wonderfully warm and giving because the whole thing was integrated with heating elements and somehow spiritually cushioned by a layer of living water underneath.

In the next dream, my brothers and sisters and I were renovating our parents' little white farmhouse. Mom and Dad had been deceased for many years and our beloved childhood home stopped being the heart of our family gatherings when they died. In the dream, we were all there, Mom and Dad were alive and I exclaimed, "Look, Dad, if we take out the kitchen wall and open it to the living room, you can see right through! We'll make the living room into a dining room, take out the bedroom wall and make that the living room and then, *look Dad, you can see right through!"* We began taking the walls down, all of us helping. As the house opened up, it became absolutely beautiful. Like the church dream, it was also much larger than life.

The third dream was about our family barn which had been a source of pure magic for me as a child. I knew every nook and cranny, named all the cats, horses and cows, and spent hours day-dreaming in the hay mow. In present day reality, the barn has since fallen into ruin with the roof fallen in. In the dream, however, the barn was acres big, filled with happy animals and it even had many apartments in it for people to live in. I remember being in charge of caretaking as I instructed a young man who was moving in how to care for the animals and general upkeep.

In the fourth dream, I dreamt about a friend's childhood home that I had visited often as a young girl. In the dream, the house was again much larger than it is in reality, filled with wondrous rooms for each person. My friend and her whole family were in the dream as we made passionate plans regarding important community and political issues that we felt called to be a part of.

In all these encouraging dreams, there is expansion and rebuild-ing going on beneath the scenes and a sense that things are never quite what they seem; life is fuller, wider and much broader than what we see with our eyes. Four stages emerge: the need for com-fort and warmth as new beginnings are being made, opening up as walls are taken down to increase inner scope, next comes the desire for caretaking and instructing others how to do the same, and last-ly, finding one's role in the web of life beyond one's own small world. For wounded or broken-hearted persons, *the dreams suggest that life is literally infused with a continuance that restores and renews our lives through its own momentum.* This phenomenon is not of our own making in any way; God does all the work and recreating. Our only job is to be present, to show up—until we become ready and able to respond and participate, one small step at a time.

Honeycomb God of Unfinished Spaces in Our Souls, remind us that when we feel sad and empty, spiritual creativity—like air which can't be seen or felt—immediately flows energy into the architecture of our hope.

30

✿ Celebrating Life and Love ✿

Love is patient; love is kind; love is not envious or boast-
ful or arrogant or rude. It does not insist on its own way;
it is not irritable or resentful; . . .it bears all things,
believes all things, hopes all things, endures all things.
Love never ends.   1 Corinthians 13:4,5,7,8a

BIRTHDAYS . . . how does a survivor who has lost a loved one to suicide face them? Each year, when our birthdays arrive, we are reminded that our loved one is not here to celebrate with us. Each year, we grow one year older while our loved one who died remains in our memory the age they were when they died. We miss them terribly.

How then, should we view our birthdays? When I turned 50 years of age, the theme quote that became significant to me was, "We can do no great things, only small things with great love," by Mother Teresa. As I reflected and looked back on the last decade of my life, its message rang with clarity—not as a romanticized, sentimental or naïve philosophy, but as a powerful and healing way of approaching life. I wrote:

"In the time span of the last ten years, I lost my health, had a number of surgeries—one of which left me with a permanently paralyzed face, officially became a disabled person and lost a beloved child to probable suicide when I was 47. What comes to mind when I think of the horrendous things I've endured is the phrase, 'I survived.' I echo this from poignant comments I once heard residents in a nursing home make when asked what they are most proud of in life. In his book, *The Power of Myth,* Joseph Campbell explains that he believes people are not so much seeking meaning in life as the experience of feeling fully alive. [1] It has come as a shock to me that it is possible to feel fully alive and in love with life after knowing tragedy yet, time and time again, I witness the reality of this in the lives of others who have known severe hardship and trauma of many kinds. I have come to view Campbell's words as a universal invitation.

"Something shining emerges through those who say yes to life and helping others. The pain transforms and gifts reveal themselves. Author Macrina Wiederkehr writes, *'if you want to know if you are good for others, ask yourself how much hope you've given them.'* [2] I find that the dynamics of this hope seem to rise and fall like breathing; it results from first having been supported and comforted myself and then extending what I've received. Friend and author, Ave Clark, refers to holy resilience. Learning to live from the heart, being able to embrace both the darkness of suffering and grief and the light of hope illustrates the delicate balance this entails. Clarissa Pinkola Estes, Ph.D. states that there are three things that differentiate living from the soul versus living from the ego: '. . . *the ability to sense and learn new ways, the tenacity to ride a rough road and the patience to learn deep love over time.'* [3]

"The tremendous patience required defies words. As Katherine Mansfield once wrote, *'Everything in life that we accept undergoes a change. So suffering must become Love. This is the mystery. This is what I must do. I must pass from personal love to greater love.'* [4] On days when grief is wrenching and we are worn out, done in and used up from adversity and suffering, this concept can feel like an impossibility. As my lovely husband described it once (referring to his own journey), 'I sometimes get my blessings confused with my burdens.' It is then somehow, that the mystery of grace enables us to regroup. We remind ourselves what is important and what we hold as truth.

"For me, that means remembering that I am a spiritual being on a human journey, not the other way around. That I live a life steeped in the love of friends and family, that happiness is not my goal (as in worldly things that pass away) but rather, understanding that joy, satisfaction and passion for my work bring me peace and purpose. As I count my blessings and approach 50 years of age, I feel lucky. Lucky to be here, lucky to be contributing something worthwhile to the world and lucky to be continually learning that doing small things with great love is what living, healing and being is all about."

God of Deepest Love, each year that we celebrate the day we were born, we celebrate our existence. Each year that we honor the birthday of loved ones who have died, we still commemorate the same thing. Death doesn't change it, but rather, enlarges and deepens our understanding of what a birthday really means.

31

༄ Lavender Hearts ༄

. . . and I will write it on their hearts; and I will be their God and they shall be my people. Jeremiah 31:33

I WAS going through some long-forgotten files when, in the bottom drawer way at the back, I found a fat folder, brimming with about four dozen meditations I'd written when our sons were young. It was ironic because just that morning I had received an essay assignment from a friend, who asked, *"How does God mother you?"* After spending an hour reading through the folder, I went out to sit in a lawn chair, poignantly wondering: Those small boys, all grown up, where did they go? The memories seemed like only yesterday—clear and shining—like I could just step right back into those luminous days. On the other hand, they also seemed hazy and condensed to ethereal, filmy vestiges of a different lifetime.

Holding the file of those fledgling days was like holding my own motherhood in my hands; like going back in time and blessing who I was as a young woman, blessing my family and consecrating that era when the boys were growing up and I and my husband were growing up right along with them. As I did the blessing rite of passage, it was also like an initiation because I was moving into yet another new period in my life as the mother of adult children and a woman with a life of her own soon to turn fifty years of age.

The first emotion I felt was astonishment at all the memories I'd captured in writing. As I read the first essay, I felt elated that I had done it and also shocked that so much of it was forgotten. For some reason, I had written, "Life is a process of deepening and shifting. Change in itself is inevitable, but we have the choice of changing with God or without. More often than not, we find ourselves in places and times that we never would have envisioned would be ours, and circumstances beyond our control teach us painful truths we would have chosen not to learn . . . yet each day shapes us and takes us one more step toward eternity." I began writing down my present day responses to words I'd written nearly two decades ago. I was surprised, because my initial intent in reading the old memories was to prayerfully bless and uphold who I'd been as a new mother unseasoned by life. Paradoxically, however, I found that the spirited, earnest voice of myself as a young woman had much to say to the present me, offering life-giving and even prophetic words regarding the grief I was experiencing in the loss of our son. There was a mothering synergy between who I was, who I am and who I will become that was nurturing and unexpected.

Themes of love, sacrifice, wounds transformed, happiness and gifts offered up for others were common threads throughout all four dozen anecdotes. Those early expressions of faith were filled with idealistic aspirations that now, as a middle-aged woman, I still believe but comprehend on a much deeper level. One of my favorite essays described a raging snowstorm during which my husband and sons had all come down with the flu at the same time, and I was completely overwhelmed with caregiver duties. Done in with worry and caring for them, I felt used up and ready to pull my hair out. In the middle of the night, when everyone was sleeping, I was suddenly brimming with a need to paint. I designed a stencil pattern and taking lavender paint, stenciled hearts all the way across a 20-foot beam that spanned our living room. As I worked, joy filled me, bringing a welcome respite from all the stress. For years to come, I had that heart-strewn beam to remind me of the creativity that can passionately rise out of the devotion we have for our families when life is hard. Twenty years later, whenever I see a lavender heart, it still remains one of my favorite symbols of love, patience and endurance.

God Who Inspires Lavender Hearts in the Middle of Snowstorms, the words You write on the beams of our hearts are "made for joy." The older we get, the more it transforms and comforts us, when we need it most.

32

❧ A Letter to Adult Sons ❧

And a voice came from heaven, "You are my Son, the Beloved; with you I am well pleased." Mark 1:11

SOMETIMES, when adult children leave home and the family dynamics change, staying connected and understanding one another can be a challenge. The following letter is one I wrote to our two sons who were in their early and middle twenties, when our family's grief was about two years old.

"Dearest Boys; I don't think I've ever written the two of you a 'mother-sons' letter, and thought I would like to do that. Perhaps it's been a while since I've told you how proud I am of both of you and the directions your lives are taking. I know you are both trying your very best in life and I wanted you to know that I see it; sometimes I watch you without your knowing it and I remember when you were small. I remember what you both looked like when you were Little Mooky Man and Yellow Chicky Boy . . . and sometimes, I wish I could go back in time to those days before tragedy struck our lives and your little brother died. You both show such courage and endurance in your own unique ways; you have had to deal with far more than many boys your age.

"Looking back causes me to recall my own dear parents. I think of how who they were has influenced who I am—just as who your dad and I are shapes who you are becoming in many ways. I remember when my dad was dying. I was only twenty-two and I felt like the world was falling apart. I remember how I wanted to give my dad a hug since we never did that in my family. My parents were gentle, non-demonstrative people completely devoted to their children. I wrote dad a funny letter to say I was going to give him a hug, because I was uncomfortable to just do it without saying 'get ready,' first! Sharing this helps you understand the deeper roots of why I always like to give you hugs because it links me to my own parents.

"Then, my mom was dying not too many years later. You three boys were so young and life was thrown into crisis again. By then, I was also becoming ill and had so little stamina, it made coping doubly hard. I had to leave you boys with Grandma and Grandpa Woelfel, who took very good care of you, to be with my mom; I missed you so and I'm sure you felt confused. *Now, I realize what a tenuous paradox life is; how complex and fragile 'underneath' emotions and relationships can be—as well as solid and dependable—at the same time.* I find that 'forgiveness' is a secret to life, just as much as gratitude. This includes forgiving myself (and asking for yours) for my shortcomings, you for yours (we all have them), and both thanking, forgiving and embracing my own dear parents for the abundance of unconditional love and human limitations they had in raising me.

"It's like you boys, Jen, Rachel, your dad and I are starting our lives all over again from the ground up. As a family, we are all moving forward into the unknown, none of us knowing what the future holds for us. Dad and I love you all so much; I am sorry for the times we forgot to tell you or got preoccupied with our own grief, pursuits and problems. We are truly imperfect. Parents can sometimes fall short of the expectations of their children . . . but one day, the children realize the parents did the best they could and are just people trying to survive, like they are. Thank you for your understanding of this—wise beyond your years. Now, I wish that I could be a parent to my own parents. I wish that I could soothe them—when they were afraid, full of anxiety and didn't know what to do in life. I wish that I could reach out to them and have long, comforting conversations with them. Someday, when you are older, you will feel the same because this is part of the circle of life.

"Thank you also for remembering that Dad and I would never intentionally disappoint you. The two things I hope we can always have as a family are communication and togetherness in spirit, each in our own unique, diverse ways. Dad and I are very proud of the life partners you have found. This letter is written to the four of you out of pride and *celebrating all of us being adults together as friends.* We hope that all your dreams come true and that you find happiness, security, fulfillment and peace in life. We will always, always love you all, Mom.

"P.S. By the way, I did give my dad his hug, and more than once. And my mom, too."

God of All Parents Who are Someone's Child, life is a continuous, beautiful cycle of learning to parent others while eternally being a child at heart yourself, as well as an adult in spirit.

33

❧ The Ten Gifts of Grief ❧

So we can say with confidence, "The Lord is my helper; I will not be afraid. What can anyone do to me? Jesus Christ is the same yesterday, today and forever."

Hebrews 13:6,8

WHEN a loved one is lost to suicide, those left behind often feel the future is lost to them. They also find themselves re-evaluating the past with the loved one and questioning what they held as truth and reality. Everything they felt they could be sure of before now seems changed. They wonder, "What can I hold on to? Can I ever be sure of anything again?" Those who have made the journey find that there is an *initiation* that takes place which ushers in at least ten gifts of grief. While each concept is unique for the person experiencing it, in some dimension, these gifts are something a survivor of suicide can be sure of:

1. The re-emergence of genuine laughter and wit, not only in oneself but in family members and friends who are also grieving. Wonder fills you when this happens and you recognize it for the miracle that it is.

2. A whole new appreciation arrives for the relief and blessing of simplicity and ordinary days, rather than the anguish of "unordinary" early grief. Life finds a new rhythm.

3. New friends come into your life who understand you and who you can be authentic with.

4. There is a new depth of spirituality that is real, wrought through struggle that can embrace doubt and every layer of emotion. You learn what it means to be mighty in spirit.

5. Pride in the ability to endure is birthed in ways you never thought possible.

6. True satisfaction in performing tasks returns, such as brewing a fresh pot of coffee and relishing the fragrance that permeates the house.

7. Freedom to be oneself emerges—old inhibitions become much less important. There is a new clarity that helps you recognize what has not been life-giving to you in the past.

8. Heightened understanding and identifying with the suffering of others arrive along with the desire to offer comfort.

9. There is a new awareness of the responsibility to self-care and to honor personal limitations and boundaries.

10. Adventure is redefined into a sacred realm of vision that you never understood before. You find that it is possible to awaken thinking, "What good thing will happen today?" rather than ". . . another day of despair."

Within all these gifts comes the comprehension that grief is circular. As the years go by, you find that you can fall asleep with a tear in your eye and wake with a tear in your eye because you miss your loved one so much, and that never changes, but your heart has the potential to grow larger. You become like a chamber of countless, unending rooms that has space for every sorrow, every memory of joy and every revelation of love yet to be revealed.

God of Our Past, Present and Future, thank You for promising that we can always be sure of You.

34

✳ Ancient Dreams, Timeless Truth ✳

*I the Lord make myself known to them in visions; I
speak to them in dreams.*   Numbers 12:6b

THE Bible is seamlessly infused with people who had dreams.
One of the most powerful, brilliant dreams ever recorded,
(Genesis 28:11-12) portrays Jacob's dream of a ladder to heaven:
"He came to a certain place and stayed there for the night, because
the sun had set. Taking one of the stones of that place, he put it
under his head and lay down in that place. And he dreamed that
there was a ladder set up on the earth, the top of it reaching to
heaven; and the angels of God were ascending and descending on
it." When Jacob woke from his dream, he said, "Surely the Lord is
in this place—and I did not know it! (v. 16)"

For many survivors of suicide, the dream world takes on a
whole new dimension, linking the grieving person to the pain they
are experiencing, the memories they've had and the hope (or lack
of it) that they have for the future. The dreams become like an
ascending and descending stairway that reflects the many emotional, psychological and spiritual steps being worked through.
Some survivors, in their deep distress, ask for a sign that will let
them know that their loved one is OK and if there even is a heav-
en. They want the truth and no platitudes. They want reality that
will comfort. Numerous survivors report having at least one or
more dreams (among all the other 'emotional-processing' dreams)
that seem to carry a special spiritual message of consolation. I had

a dream like that when I was having an agonizing spell of doubting whether our son was OK and if there really is life after death.

I dreamt that Mic and I were on a glacier mountain top, where below, deep in a valley, we could clearly see the footprints of my husband and family, who had trekked to a distant village of ice houses to go fishing. However, my son and I did not have a way to get down the steep, snow covered mountain side to join them. As we were standing there pondering what to do, our son accidentally slipped over the edge as the ledge gave way. I had swathed him in a blanket from head to toe to keep him warm, and as the avalanche caught him, he went careening down the mountain. Fear clutched my heart because I was still holding the end of the blanket, knowing he would just slip out of it and be gone forever. However, to my amazement, the blanket suddenly stretched as if it were elasticized, and our son slid effortlessly all the way down to the foot of the cliff with me still holding the other end. By the time he reached the bottom, he became engulfed in powdery snow and I could not see him because the momentum caused him to slide beneath it unharmed, just under the surface. Throughout the whole dream, Mic was laughing uproariously, like he did when he was having a blast, laughing like he was having the ride of his life— a grand adventure. Then, I woke up.

When the dream ended, it was almost as if my son's dear familiar laughter lingered in my room. Through faith and my heart, I interpreted the dream to imply that our son's spirit is just beneath the surface, close by, within a different dimension that is very real, even though I can't see it or him. The blanket stretching suggests to me that I am not cut off from my son, I am still connected to him by eternal bonds of spirit and love. Most importantly, in the dream it was I who was afraid; Mic was filled with vitality. Like

Jacob who saw the incredible ladder assuring us that there is a heaven, we are each—in our own way—invited to understand that within our grief, *surely God is in this place even when we don't know it* . . . and that our loved ones' spirits never stop blessing us.

God of Ancient and Present-Day Dreamers, Your time-less word prevails, "look up . . . lighten up . . . and laugh a little."

35

❧ Expect Great Things ❧

. . . no eye has seen, nor ear heard
Nor the human heart conceived,
What God has prepared for those who love him.

1 Corinthians 2:9a

COINCIDENCES, chance encounters, messages from unlikely people . . . how little we pay attention to these forgotten avenues through which God reaches out to us. When we have lost a loved one to suicide, as we grieve and process our loss, there comes a day when our hearts heal enough to notice the world around us again. We have new eyes and ears with which to understand the revelations of love, life and God—with new capabilities we never thought could be possible for us. Through the spiritual art of "paying attention" the world gradually comes alive again—brimming with promise, comfort, guidance and messages.

This was illustrated powerfully one Christmas holiday for my husband and I. There we were, doing last minute shopping in a local, nostalgic town. The night was magical—blustery and windy enough to sway the giant evergreen swags strung across the streets, causing the lights to blink and ribbons to rustle. Exhausted holiday shoppers sped down the street, collars upturned . . . and no one looked too happy. My husband and I, in our own private world of grief (the kind that feels like a sob just below the surface while you're smiling on the outside) went about the business of finding just the right gift for the right person on our rather lengthy list.

Finally, nearly done, we had time for just one more shop before the stores closed. As we walked into the brightly lit, pine-scented store, a trendy-looking elderly woman in a red parka with snow white hair caught my eye and we nodded hello. Intensely focused on my list, I immediately forgot about her. My husband however, ended up in line at the cash register with her, holding all the merchandise I was buying. He immediately struck up a conversation and I could hear them talking. She was saying, " . . .so, I was talking to God the other day about my big mouth . . . and God said, 'So what—you gotta say what needs to be said,' " while my husband, who loves outspoken, eccentric people chuckled. She was very attuned to him and he ended up telling her that we'd lost a son to suicide. By now, the young clerk and other customers were also listening closely. Expressing heartfelt sympathy, the elderly woman told my husband how sorry she was and praised him for going back to college and re-creating his life.

The solicitous clerk rang up our purchases, and as we said Merry Christmas to the elderly woman and walked out of the store, she called, *"Expect great things!"* Out on the side walk, I caught my husband's arm, and thoroughly struck by what the woman said, jested, "Did we just encounter an angel on earth?" For someone to tell us—parents who had lost a child to suicide— to expect great things seemed utterly preposterous. But why did it feel so right, needed and heavenly to hear?

The next day, the prophetic message seemed to echo in my mind. I could not forget it. Taking a pen, I tenderly scrawled the words on a sheet of paper and taped them to our sliding glass door. Then, my husband and I went forward in our lives . . . helping each other and others to believe it, one day at a time.

God Who Speaks through Earth Angels, You remind us every day that despite our pain, You promise us great comfort for our hearts, great love in our lives and glad tidings which will bring us great joy not only on Christmas morning but all our lives through.

36

ஃ How We Pray Now ஃ

These things I remember as I pour out my soul; . . .
By day the Lord commands his steadfast love,
and at night his song is with me, a prayer to the God
of my life. Psalm 42:4, 8

SOMETIMES, survivors of suicide are so changed by their loss, that even their prayer life undergoes a metamorphosis. When I posed the question to a community of friends on our web site message board, *"How do you pray?"* their responses amazed me. Ann began by sharing a quote from C.S. Lewis, "The prayer preceding all prayer is 'May it be the real I who speaks. May it be the real Thou that I speak to.'" Ann continued, "All prayer is sacred and is one's personal soul talking to God in the most honest and open way that a human can ever do with another being or spirit. I love prayer; to me, it is a cleansing of my heart and mind, it is what keeps me grounded and sane in a sometimes insane world. It is my strength when I am weak and weary; it reminds me that with God I can do all things, even bear illness and grief." Ann, who has begun keeping a prayer journal says she does this because "when my talks with God get so intense and deep, I actually can feel His presence in my room. Afterwards, I note down all that I feel, all that I question, all that 'I hear from God' at that moment when He comforts, guides and holds me close to Him. What a beautiful joy this practice is for me, it is truly a new gift."

Sharon Allard wrote, "When people speak of the power of prayer, I sometimes wonder if they really understand how powerful it can be when we get out of the way and let God pray in us. To me, it is as simple as allowing God to live more and more fully within you. He does the healing, He does the loving, He brings us together in our shattered state." She beautifully clarified, ". . . for me, the hush of prayer comes late at night, when everyone is finally asleep and I can forget about all the hustle and bustle, lie down and snuggle under my quilt, feeling my aching body sink into the bed and the warmth spreading through me; as my heart and mind turn fully to God (as much as I am capable of), I realize how blessed I am because I can seek that peace whenever I so choose. I hold it ardently to my heart and fall asleep praying to love the world with God's own love."

My husband wrote, "I have a notion that prayer is like a huge blanket of good, protection, guidance, comfort and consolation that is present in our lives. This blanket is for everyone and everyone can contribute to it. When our son died, I knew that nothing could reverse his death physically. However, in my darkest hour, I did not stop praying even though I felt crushed and empty inside. Now, three years later, I can see that my prayers have, in a small way, lifted me to the point of using my experience to benefit others. I see prayer as an energy source our spirit requires—just as our bodies need food for sustaining health and strength. I never truly realized what 'beseeching from the heart' meant until my son died; I am not ashamed to say how broken and dependent upon God and others I was for a long time after it happened. Before my son's death, I had been a student of prayer, but had never been able to absorb what was the essence of prayer. Now, I try to live it."

Libbie Adams expanded, "For so many years, prayer was a mystery to me, too. What good did it do to say words to God, when I felt He already knew the desire of my heart? And why ask for something specific, when I felt I wasn't wise enough about any given situation to make that kind of request? I began to see prayer as two-sided. Either it was asking for or about something or it was giving thanks for or about something. Eventually, for me, prayer began to be a way of joining my spiritual energy with God's and with all other people who were also praying. I would sit in silence, visualizing the person I was praying for, and seeing them cloaked in Love and Light, in Peace and Health, in Wisdom and Understanding."

Dee Frye wrote of "letting go and letting God" and described her way, "I, too, keep my prayers simple. I keep a list, (mostly on post-its!) and lift people up; as prayers are answered, I send up thankful praises. While I drive to and from work or school, I talk to God like a friend. One of my favorite quotes comes from Samuel Taylor Coleridge, 'He prayeth best who loveth best/ All things both great and small;/ For the dear God who loveth us,/ He made and loveth all.' "

Other people write of discovering dimensions to prayer that are connected to memories. I remembered a time when my childhood best friend, Judy Olson and I were about 8 years old. Judy had come to the farm where I lived, to play. It was ungodly windy, the kind of wind so powerful it laid the corn flat and practically knocked us off our feet. We walked down the short gravel driveway to the clover meadow across the road from the mailbox. There, Dad and Grandpa had stacked huge towers of baled hay—as tall as a house—it seemed to Judy and me because we were so small. Windswept all the way, we plopped down with our backs against the bales, sitting with our feet splayed, grinning. It was like the world went still. There was no wind at all because we were protected from its force by the fragrant bales of hay. Safe in this small, pleasant pocket of quiet, Judy and I whiled away the afternoon in delight. The memory reminds me to believe in magic, life, friendship and all the sacred, eternal things that will always be ours, no matter what heartbreak we must endure. It is as if the memory prays in me with a language all its own all these years later, emphasizing, as Elijah discovered, that God responds to our prayers out of the winds of grief and chaos with a still small voice that we can count on.

God Who Understands Every Language of the Heart Known to Humankind, as You call us to intimacy, familiarity and complete freedom to be ourselves with you, we revel in the truth that there is no right or wrong way to pray. That's the beauty of it.

37

❧ The Circle of Life ❧

It is he who sits above the circle of the earth, . . . He gives power to the faint, and strengthens the powerless.

Isaiah 40:22a, 29

ANCIENT scholars describe the soul as a circle, a universal symbol of completeness and totality with no beginning and no end. The circle represents all the never-ending cycles and seasons of life as well as the birth, death and rebirth of the journey from the womb to the tomb and back to the womb of everlasting life.

I have a beautiful necklace that is a treasure to me. A gift from a friend who lost a child, it consists simply and elegantly of three circles within one another, suspended on a gold chain. I wear it in memory of our son who died, a special symbol of comfort that enfolds many layers of meaning to me.

It also serves to remind me that when we come full circle in life, we come to an understanding of what it means to give of ourselves so that others might live and flourish. This message is clearly our greatest hope. As we process our challenges through faith, we come full circle into the fullness of God's life within us. We learn that God does not want us to live with worry, despair and fear as hounds at our heels or as a cold hand at our backs. As we discover new life within and beyond our struggles, we are able to channel it for the sake of others. Never was this illustrated more powerfully than through the life and death of our friend, Sharon, who died the day after I finished my interviews with her for this book.

There were four of us: Sharon, Ann, Libbie and myself, all friends who met on our web site. We knew Sharon was dying. She'd suffered a massive heart attack and was existing precariously on nitro-glycerin and oxygen. Doctors had not expected her to live, but month after month she lingered. As her physical body faded, her voice of wisdom grew stronger and stronger. As a circle of friends, we grew as close to Sharon as I believe it is possible to be with a soul friend on this earth, each in our own unique way.

Because Sharon's words were so compelling and expansive, I think I forgot she was dying. She had such passion and her words were filled with inner vitality, amazing creativity, descriptions and expression of her life's joys, sorrows and wounds. She held nothing back. As a member of our core group, she made many friends and was devoted to ministering on our web site, reaching out to others with uncommon honesty, humor, depth and commitment, even when she was so ill she could barely leave her bed. And yet, she was so ready to die. She had a profound sense of eternity and the welcoming arms of God and longed to write of it . . . and often did, to all of us. We were not prepared when we got the word that she had died rather quickly in her husband's arms. She had prepared us as best she could, there was nothing left unsaid, but it was heartbreaking to let her go. Just a few nights before she died, I had a dream of an amazing cloud overhead that transformed into hundreds of wings. After Sharon died, I thought of freedom and the dream. Sharon was free.

But we three friends left behind felt such a hole in our little circle. We were left to carry on, knowing we would never hear her voice again in the way in which we were accustomed. There had been such a connection between us. Through Sharon, we learned what it means to be a mentor even in death. I asked Libbie and Ann what that meant to them and they both said the same thing. Libbie who writes for Guideposts wrote, " . . .*it means having your life be the example of your beliefs, sharing your thoughts and experiences with someone else but not forcing them to embrace your truths. It means being a teacher rather than a preacher, willing to give guidance and yet to know where the line is between guiding and leading.*" Ann eloquently wrote, "*A mentor is just being the best example of whatever you are trying to mentor the person about, being as honest and authentic as you can be, that is how another learns from you.*"

Sharon had a very special place in her heart for survivors of suicide and her last gift to us all is as our mentor in teaching us not only how to die but more importantly, how to live, grieve and integrate all that we are. She taught us what it means to come full circle as a human being and a spiritual being. Blessed be her beautiful memory.

Creator God Who is the Nucleus of Every Cell and Every Soul, may the wholeness of Your love come full circle in us.

38

❧ From Generation to Generation ❧

For the Lord is good; His steadfast love endures forever,
and his faithfulness to all generations.   Psalm 100:5

PRECEDING the front page advertisements of *"Cold Foods for
Hot Weather: Sardines—Teenie Weenie 2 for 25¢* and *Macaroni for
salads, 5¢ a package"—The Daily Gazette's* (Thursday, August 11,
1932) headline reads: **Head of Closed Bank at Vesta Is Suicide.**
The opening paragraph states, "Charles Boushek, 67, president of
the closed Vesta bank, was found dead Wednesday night on his
son's farm one mile east of Vesta where he had taken his life by
hanging, probably after taking poison." [5] This man was my husband's great-grandfather.

According to sources gathered from the time, Charles had been
in failing health for several years and his family had urged him to
seek rest and help in a hospital. Charles had resisted the idea, holding on to hope that he would get better, stating that he did not
want to leave his home, family or the land that he loved; however,
he had finally agreed to go to the hospital the following weekend.
Those plans never materialized as he took his own life on August
10, 1932, thereby becoming another face of suicide.

We study the dignified, formal photos we have of him, with his
lovely wife, two daughters and seven sons. He is a handsome man,
dressed in a dark, well-cut suit, white shirt and tie with a watch
chain draping out of his lapeled vest. Through other newspaper
articles and his obituary, my husband and I learned that Charles

was born in Bohemia on May 27, 1868. When he was twelve, he moved to this country and settled in New York where he learned the tailoring trade. He was married to Katrina Kotval on August 10, 1886 when he was eighteen years old. As his story begins forming in our imaginations, we realize that he killed himself on the day of his forty-sixth wedding anniversary.

Through further investigation, we discovered that he was prominent in the Vesta community affairs, was deeply respected, had served as mayor and had many friends all over the county. Through reflection, the events that led to his suicide come alive, taking us back to another time and place: It had to have been hot, it was August. Like many banks during the depression, the Vesta bank went under, already in trouble before Charles was at the helm. The anguish of seeing friends, neighbors and family lose money weighed heavily on Charles, a man of great integrity, as well as the futility of knowing there was nothing he could do about the situation. Family members became more and more concerned, saying that he was "not right" as one put it, as he struggled to deal with the stress. Yet, he appeared to have rallied somewhat and seemed a little better, by some accounts.

Statistics teach us that men are four times more likely to die by suicide than women and that elderly men have the highest suicide rates. Also, some studies relate that there can be a hereditary link. According to SAVE (Suicide Awareness Voices of Education), "95% of suicides are caused by brain diseases such as clinical depression, anxiety disorders, bipolar illness and schizophrenia" (which can often carry a genetic predisposition from one generation to the next). My husband and I can't help but wonder about a possible genetic link between our Mic and Charles, who committed suicide 67 years apart.

It is important to us to tell Charles's story and to let our compassion and the family's pride in who he was as a person be the tie that binds rather than how he died. His obituary, ahead of its time in depth and enlightenment reads, "Understanding his condition as his family did, although their hearts are heavy with sorrow, his act is forgiven and they only try to remember the loving things he did for all of them while in good health. He will be greatly missed."

A poem entitled *In Memory of Dad,* also printed in the obituary at the time, poignantly expressed the family's sentiments, speaking for many sons and daughters who have lost a parent to suicide:

> Not now, but in the coming years,
> It may be in the better land,
> We'll read the meaning of our tears,
> And there sometime we'll understand,
> We'll catch the broken thread again,
> And finish what we here began,
> Heaven will
> all mysteries explain,
> And then, Ah then, we'll understand.
> Dear old Dad, with a heart of gold,
> Tho' we miss you from our midst,
> We'll struggle bravely on, hoping,
> Someday we too will understand.

Faith, as our universal language, teaches us that when we die we are met by friends and relatives who have died who are there to welcome us home and to offer comfort. We believe that Charles was among the first ones there waiting for Mic and surely, his first words were, "It'll all be fine, Son."

Faithful God of our Ancestors, thank You with all our hearts that from generation to generation we can be there for each other in both life and death, and that in You, the threads of love and understanding are never truly broken.

39

❧ Mic's Message: Two Years Later ❧

*And they went out and proclaimed the good news every-
where, while the Lord worked with them and confirmed
the message by the signs that accompanied it.*

Mark 16:20

IN an old *Christopher News Note* that I've saved, it says that
a joyful life begins with three things: a deep appreciation of
God's love, a noble purpose in life and a spirit of fidelity to the
duties of the present moment. [6] These affirming words came to
me when I founded a new web site for my husband on the second anniversary of our son's death. Indeed . . . a joyful life . . .
how can there be such a thing when a parent has lost a beloved
child to probable suicide?

In *Coincidences: Touched by a Miracle,* Antoinette Bosco writes,
"I have always believed that we are in touch with our loved ones
who have died. It was the beautiful teaching of the Communion
of Saints that gave me this assuring sense that we are all connected to one another. But it was only after experiencing the deaths of
loved ones that I had what I call 'gifts' of feeling their presence . .
.sometimes through a sign that seemed only coincidental at
first." [7]

And thus it was for me also, that out of the most wrenching pain
a person can know, rising out of the most shattering questions, that
I was ushered into a completely new world that I never even knew
existed before. Antoinette writes in her book that there is a "pat-

tern or a guidance of people and the world toward a higher purpose and that we can tap into this if we respond to grace." For me, that journey took approximately two years of incubation, grieving and processing. As the second anniversary of our son's death approached, I dreamt that our son was with my husband and I in our living room. He was happy and natural and had his hands hidden behind his back, grinning. I playfully grabbed his hands and pulling them open, found that they were empty! This poignant dream seemed to affirm the realization that although our son's hands are empty because his work on earth is done . . . my hands and my husband's are not empty. We (as all people) are called to that higher purpose that founds itself on Romans 8:28.

And so it was that I felt it was time to act. I contacted a friend, Gary Frye, who is a web builder/designer and asked him if he'd help me establish a support web site for teen/adult depression and suicide prevention. Without hesitation, he said yes. We worked closely as a team, with me doing the text writing and him doing the graphics and mechanical creating. We felt as if we were conduits or channels of something wonderful revealing itself as coincidences seemed to affirm the work we were doing. Within days, our site, "Mic's Message" became a reality. By the third week, we had over a thousand hits to our site and over 150 posted messages.

Most importantly, because of the message board, we have a place where people of all ages and walks of life can gather to offer solidarity, share questions, insights, pain, triumphs and comfort as trusted friends. Surprisingly, people who frequent message boards quickly become creative and adept at projecting personality and self-expression through web language. There is a certain freedom to be oneself and to get to the heart of a matter. Sometimes, a support web site is all some people have as a safe place where they can go for comfort and expression. At its very least, a successful web site can be a warm place of temporary shelter for someone passing through. At its deepest level, it becomes a sacred community— that, as the old *Christopher Note* suggested—is based on a deep appreciation of God's love, a sense of a purpose and meaning in life and learning to live in the fragile, precious, present moment in time . . . as survivors supporting survivors. *Through the creation of Mic's Message, my husband and I began to truly grasp what it means to walk in the world for loved ones who have died.*

God of Peace, Passion and Purpose, not only is life in You infused with love and comfort . . . You unite us to our loved ones who have passed over in order to heal our- selves and the world through giving.

Conclusion

❧ *Revelations of Love* ❧

On February 5, 2002, I wrote the following poem to Mic:

What Our Hearts Become
Tears still come
And we have spells of feeling
We cannot go on without you . . .
That surely, you cannot be gone.

We are like Genesis now
Our hearts burgeoning planets
As grief moves over the face of the waters
Bringing to life whole new continents
Climates
And atmospheres in us.

God's gift to us . . .
So that we are not destroyed
By the wretched confines of grief
But rather enlarged
While love surrounds us.

Another tear falls
And behold
An island is born.

Adolfo Quezada writes, "We were born into the world to give
and receive love on behalf of God. We are here because it is 'here'
that we are one with God. Conscious living means conscious loving. This begins with love for ourselves. As we love and honor our
physical selves, we strive for the physical welfare of others. As we

respond to our emotional needs, we respond to the emotional needs of others. As we open ourselves to the realm of the spirit, we encourage others to open as well. Above all . . . we allow God to live through us according to our uniqueness."

Adolfo believes that to live consciously is to live deliberately, with purpose and meaning, to drink in the wonder of creation through our senses and to unleash the divine creativity that finds its expression in and through us. In other words, to receive and offer revelations of love as we are gifted with them.

Writing this book has been an experience of that concept. The book practically seemed to write itself through three avenues: the *outpouring* of my own grief, the *gathering* of other people's stories and the *channeling* of many ideas, co-incidences and insights that seemed to filter through me with a momentum of their own. I no longer felt like I was a well of tears, but a wellspring of comfort and consolation that seemed to pour through me; even on days when I was too weary to feel it, it was still a reality. As I told several friends, it was like this book put its arms around the people I care about and who care about me—as one by one, beloved friends, colleagues and family offered their earnest, deepest thoughts to me. Sometimes I would feel so humbled, honored and amazed—moved to tears—by the generosity and beauty in the soul work of others. As my writing came to a close and I was able to look back at the three-year journey this book entailed, I began to realize that each unique offering from others, along with divine inspiration, were like pearls dropping into my lap—adding to the string of pearls I'd already been given. Writing this book became my pearl of great price.

The cover image for this book, by Sister Mary Southard, CSJ, entitled *The Child Comes* depicts dimensions beyond words. When I showed the image to my friend, Ann, she wrote, ". . . I see so much in that picture. I see all parents holding their beloved children, I see you looking for Mic and finding him at night when the earth is at its darkest. I see Mother Earth holding all of us in her arms; I see a sacred, loving angel holding and protecting her child, which is all of us. I see myself trying to protect those I love represented by the child, and I see the earth depicted as the pearl of great wisdom formed from a journey that is sometimes so beautiful, and yet sometimes so painful that we cannot even put words to it. All that is part of the price we pay to live, to love and to experience being on this earth as a spirit of God's creation."

The gift of this ongoing creation within us individually and collectively as we integrate the brilliant beauty in our lives as well as the pain beyond words is expressed profoundly in the following story about Lillian Meyers, a special friend of mine. Since my spirit name is Lily, I felt a special bond with her as soon as I met her. Lillian is a vibrant psychologist who, when her beloved son Jimmy died in 1981, discontinued her private practice to train other professionals to understand the grieving process. She also provides programs to bereavement groups, especially for parents, including many in Compassionate Friends, whose children died by suicide. Now in her middle seventies, Lillian continues to tirelessly and passionately carry on this work. One April day, Lillian's beautiful first born daughter, Catherine, who has been legally blind since birth and who is a poet and business analyst wrote the following reflection after she'd spent some time on the island where Lillian was born and raised and still visits. Lillian said her daughter came back from walking on the beach and wrote, *"This is my last morning of what has been a week of glorious dawn walks. I feel more peaceful than I did at the beginning of the week. I pause at the bottom of the steps for one more look. I realize again how the beach has changed in the hour I have been walking and since the week started, and since last year when I was here. And I reflect that I am not the same person I was an hour ago, or on Monday, or last year. And when next I am fortunate enough to come again, neither I nor the beach will be the same. The tide pools will change each day as the ocean cleanses what needs to be healed and brings new life continually. Whenever I begin to fear change, I will think of the tide pools accepting constant change gracefully and gratefully."*

Lillian and her daughter understand well the spirituality of islands born in each of us following the death of a loved one to suicide or any other way. The beauty of their compassion and wisdom offers guidance for each of us, reminding us that nothing stays the same except for love, which only deepens over time. Like the tide pools Catherine writes so eloquently about, the revelations of love in our lives keep shifting, cleansing, healing and bringing new life that will sustain us. We do not need to cling to it or search for it, because like the ocean, it uplifts us, embraces us and carries us. Someday, like our loved ones who have died, we ourselves will become a part of it. We will be waves and tide pools that brush up on the island shores of others still making the journey—our voices an echo of the hope of things to come.

SUICIDE: QUESTIONS MOST FREQUENTLY ASKED

Why do people kill themselves?

Most of the time people who kill themselves are very sick with depression or one of the other types of depressive illnesses, which occur when the chemicals in a person's brain get out of balance or become disrupted in some way. Healthy people do not kill themselves. A person who has depression does not think like a typical person who is feeling good. Their illness prevents them from being able to look forward to anything. They can only think about NOW and have lost the ability to imagine into the future. Many times they don't realize they are suffering from a treatable illness and they feel they can't be helped. Seeking help may not even enter their mind. They do not think of the people around them, family or friends, because of their illness. They are consumed with emotional, and many times, physical pain that becomes unbearable. They don't see any way out. They feel hopeless and helpless. They don't want to die, but it's the only way they feel their pain will end. It is a non-rational choice. Getting depressed is involuntary— no one asks for it, just like people don't ask to get cancer or diabetes. But, we do know that depression is a treatable illness that people can feel good again!

Please remember—depression, plus alcohol or drug use can be lethal. Many times people will try to alleviate the symptoms of their illness by drinking or using drugs not prescribed by doctors. Alcohol and/or drugs will make the disease worse! There is an increased risk for suicide because alcohol and drugs decrease judgment and increase impulsivity.

Do people who attempt suicide do it to prove something, to show people how bad they feel and to get sympathy?

They don't do it necessarily to prove something, but it is certainly a cry for help, which should never be ignored. This is a warning to people that something is terribly wrong. Many times people cannot express how horrible or desperate they're feeling—they simply cannot put their pain into words. There is no way to describe it. A suicide attempt must always be taken seriously. People who have attempted suicide in the past, may be at risk for trying it again and possibly completing it, if they don't get help for their depression.

Can a suicidal person mask their depression with happiness?

We know that many people suffering from depression can hide their feelings, appearing to be happy. But, can a person who is contemplating suicide feign happiness? Yes, they can. But, most of the time a suicidal person will give clues as to how desperate he/she is feeling. They may be subtle clues though, and that's why knowing what to watch for is critical. A person may "hint" that he/she is thinking about suicide. For example, they may say something like, "Everyone would be better off without me." Or, "It doesn't matter. I won't be around much longer anyway." We need to "key into" phrases like those instead of dismissing them as just talk. It is estimated that 80% of people who died of suicide, mentioned it to a friend or relative before dying. Other danger signs are having a preoccupation with death, losing interest in things one cares about, giving things away, having a lot of "accidents," or engaging in risk-taking behavior, like speeding or reckless driving, or general carelessness. Some people even joke about completing suicide. This should always be taken seriously.

Is it more likely for a person to attempt suicide if he/she has been exposed to it in their family or has had a close friend die of suicide?

We know that suicide tends to run in families, but it is believed that this is due to the fact that depression and other related depressive illnesses have a genetic component, and that if they are left untreated (or mistreated) it can result in suicide. But talking about suicide or being aware of a suicide that happened in your family or to a close friend does not put you at risk for attempting it, if you are healthy. The only people who are at risk are those who are vulnerable in the first place—vulnerable because of an illness called depression or one of the other depressive illnesses. The risk increases if the illness is not treated. It's important to remember that not all people who have depression, have suicidal thoughts—only some.

Why don't people talk about depression and suicide?

The main reason people don't talk about it is because of the stigma. People who suffer from depression are afraid that others will think they are "crazy." Society still hasn't accepted depressive illnesses like they've accepted other diseases. Alcoholism is a good example—no one ever wanted to talk openly about it but now that society views it as disease, most people feel pretty comfortable discussing it with others if it's in their family. They talk of the effect it has had on their lives and different treatment plans. And everyone is educated on the dangers of alcohol and on substance abuse prevention. As for suicide, it's a topic that has a long history of being taboo—something that should just be forgotten, kind of swept under the rug. And that's why people keep dying. Suicide is misunderstood by most people, so the myths are perpetuated. The stigma prevents people from getting help, and prevents society from learning more about suicide and depression. If everyone were educated on these subjects, many lives could be saved.

Will "talking things out" cure depression?

The studies that have been done on "talk therapy" vs. using antidepressant medication have shown that in some cases of depression, using well-supported psychotherapies, such as cognitive behavioral therapy, or interpersonal therapy, may considerably alleviate the symptoms of depression. In other cases, this simply wouldn't be enough. It would be like trying to talk a person out of having a heart attack. Studies continue to show that a combination of psychotherapy (talking therapies) and antidepressant medication is the most effective way of treating most people who suffer from depression.

Why do people attempt suicide when they appear to have been feeling so much better?

Sometimes people who are severely depressed and contemplating suicide don't have enough energy to carry it out. But, as the disease begins to "lift" they may regain some of their energy but still have feelings of hopelessness. There's also another theory that people just kind of "give in" to the anguished feelings (the disease), because they just can't fight it anymore. This in turn, releases some of their anxiety, which makes them "appear" calmer. Even if they do die by suicide, it doesn't mean they chose it. If they knew they could have the life that they had before the illness, they would choose life.

If a person's "mind is made up," can they still be stopped?

Yes! People who are contemplating suicide go back and forth, thinking about life and death. The pain can come in "waves." They don't want to die, they just want the pain to stop. Once they know they can be helped, that there are treatments available for their illness, that it isn't their fault and that they are not alone, it gives them hope. We should never "give up" on someone, just because we think they've made their mind up!

Is depression the same as the blues?

No. Depression is different from the blues. The blues are normal feelings that eventually pass, like when a good friend moves away or the disappointment that a person feels if something didn't turn out as expected. Eventually the person will feel like his old self again. But the feelings and symptoms associated with depression linger, and no matter how hard a person tries to talk him or herself into feeling better, it just won't work. People can't snap themselves out of depression. It's not a character flaw or a personal weakness and it doesn't have anything to do with willpower. It is an illness.

SAVE—Suicide Awareness Voices of Education
7317 Cahill Road, Suite 207
Minneapolis, MN 55439-2080
Phone: (952) 946-7998 — Toll Free 1-888-511-SAVE
Fax: (952) 829-0841
Word Wide Web Site: http://www.save.org
E-mail Address: save@winternet.com

Suicide Awareness Voices of Education (SAVE) is an organization dedicated to educating the public about suicide prevention.

SAVE's Recommendations for Responding to Suicide Survivors

Understand that the #1 cause of suicide is untreated depression.

Understand that 95% of suicides are caused by brain diseases such as clinical depression, anxiety disorders, bipolar illness, and schizophrenia.

Depression is a no-fault disease of the brain. It is biological and is not caused by life events such as the break-up of a relationship or loss of a job.

Tell the survivor you are sorry for his or her loss.

Do not make statements such as, "You'll marry again." "At least you have other children." These are not comforting statements. A heartfelt, "I am sorry for your loss," is appropriate.

Understand that the survivor may be experiencing an overwhelming number of intense emotions.

Shock, pain, anger, bewilderment, disbelief, yearning, anxiety, depression, and stress are emotions expressed by some but not all suicide survivors.

Remember that grief is an intensely individualistic journey.

Although you may have experienced grief in your life, do not say, "I know how you feel." You do not know how the survivor is feeling, so ask, "How are you feeling?"

Listen.

If the survivor wishes to talk, be available. Say, "This must be so very hard for you." Listening can be the most comforting thing you can do for a suicide survivor.

Be aware of suicide survivor grief support groups in your community.

Many survivors have found it very helpful to attend a suicide survivor support group. Encourage the survivor to attend at least three or four meetings.

Read the book, *Suicide: Survivors—A Guide for Those Left Behind* by Adina Wrobleski. (available by calling SAVE at 952-946-7998 x10)

Many suicide survivors have found this book to be helpful.

Grief After Suicide

- Know that you can survive. Though you may feel you cannot survive, you can.

- The intense feelings of grief can be overwhelming and frightening. This is normal. You are not going crazy; you are grieving.

- You may experience feelings of guilt, confusion, and anger, even fear. These are all common responses to grief.

- You may even have thoughts of suicide. This, too, is common. It does not mean you will act on those thoughts.

- Forgetfulness is a common, but temporary side effect. Grieving takes so much energy that other things will fade in importance.

- Keep asking "why" until you no longer need to ask.

- Healing takes time. Allow yourself the time you need to grieve.

- Grief has no predictable pattern or timetable. Though there are elements of commonality in grief, each person and each situation is unique.

- If you can delay making major decisions, do so.

- The path of grief is one of twists and turns and you may often feel you are getting nowhere.

- Remember that even setbacks are a kind of progress.

- This is the hardest thing you will ever do. Be patient with yourself.

- Seek out people who are willing to listen when you need to talk and who understand your need to be silent.

- Give yourself permission to seek professional help.

- Avoid people who try to tell you what to feel and how to feel it and, in particular, those who think you should "be over it by now."

- Find a support group for survivors that provides a safe place for you to express your feelings or simply a place to go to be with other survivors who are experiencing some of the same things you are going through.

Symptoms of Major Depression

Not all people with depression will have all these symptoms or have them to the same degree. If a person has four or more of these symptoms, if nothing can make them go away, and if they last more than two weeks, a doctor or psychiatrist should be consulted.

- Persistent sad or "empty" mood.
- Feeling hopeless, helpless, worthless, pessimistic and or guilty.
- Substance abuse.
- Fatigue or loss of interest in ordinary activities, including sex.
- Disturbances in eating and sleeping patterns.
- Irritability, increased crying, anxiety and panic attacks.
- Difficulty concentrating, remembering or making decisions.
- Thoughts of suicide, suicide plans or attempts.
- Persistent physical symptoms or pains that do not respond to treatment.

Danger Signs of Suicide

- Talking about suicide.
- Statements about hopelessness, helplessness, or worthlessness.
- Preoccupation with death.
- Suddenly happier, calmer.
- Loss of interest in things one cares about.
- Visiting or calling people one cares about.
- Making arrangements; setting one's affairs in order.
- Giving things away.

A suicidal person urgently needs to see a doctor or psychiatrist.

Notes

Part I: How Shall We Live?

Changed Forever

1. Statistics from SAVE (Suicide Awareness Voices of Education) 7317 Cahill Rd., Suite 207, Minneapolis, MN 55439 www.save.org

Why?

2. *Within These Walls,* unpublished manuscript by the late Sharon Allard. Excerpts reprinted with author's written permission.

3. Statistic from *The Journal of the American Medical Association,* SAVE.

4. Adina Wrobleski, *Suicide: Survivors, A Guide for Those Left Behind* (Minneapolis, MN: Afterwords, 1994).

An Unfailing Net

5. Excerpts used by permission from Antoinette Bosco, "Faith in Focus: Facing Questions After Suicide," *America,* August 14, 1999.

Passion Incarnate

6. Monica Furlong, *Merton: A Biography* (New York, NY: Harper & Row, Publishers, Inc., 1980).

An Important Message

7. Joyce Rupp, *Your Sorrow is My Sorrow* (New York, NY: The Crossroad Publishing Company, 1999).

Best Kept Secrets: Human Intimacy

8. Christiane Northrup, M.D., *Woman's Bodies, Woman's Wisdom: Creating Physical and Emotional Health and Healing* (New York, NY: Bantam Doubleday Dell Publishing Group, Inc., 1994).

Part II: The Task Revealed

When Grief Grows Up

1. Adolfo Quezada, *Catholic Vision,* Desert column, February, 2002.

God Applauds Self Care

2. Thomas Moore, *Care of the Soul: A Guide For Cultivating Depth and Sacredness in Everyday Life* (New York, NY: HarperCollins Publishers, 1992).

3. Julia Cameron, *The Artists Way: A Spiritual Path to Higher Creativity* (New York, NY: Jeremy P. Tarcher/Perigee Books, The Putnam Publishing Group, 1992).

A Living Compass

4. Adolfo Quezada, *Rising From the Ashes* (Totowa, NJ: Resurrection Press, Catholic Book Publishing Company, 2002).

Names of God

5. Edward M. Hays, *Prayers for a Planetary Pilgrim* (Leavenworth, KS: Forest of Peace Publishing Company, Inc, 1989).

6. Judith Duerk, *Circle of Stones, Woman's Journey to Herself* (Philadelphia, PA: Innisfree Press, Inc., 1989).

7. Thomas C. Fox, "Perspectives: Quiet Thoughts About a Friend" *National Catholic Reporter.*

Map of the Heart

8. Alla Bozarth, Julia Barkley, Terri Hawthorne, *Stars in Your Bones* (North Star Press of St. Cloud, Inc., 1990).

9. John Steinbeck, *Travels with Charley* (Penguin USA, 1981).

Floodlights of Love

10. Statistics from PFLAG website www.PFLAG.com (Parents Families Friends of Lesbians and Gays) Helpline 619-579-7640. Report of the Secretary's Task Force on Youth Suicide, U.S. Department of Health and Human Services, 1989.

11. Ibid., Taken from a study of 4,159 Massachusetts high school students. Massachusetts Youth Risk Behavior Survey (MYRBS) Department of Education, 1997.

God of the Impossible

12. Ave Clark, O.P., *Lights in the Darkness: For Survivors and Healers of Sexual Abuse* (Totowa, NJ: Resurrection Press, 1993).

Part III: A New Identity

Celebrating Life and Love

1. Joseph Campbell, *The Power of Myth: With Bill Moyers* (Anchor Books, DoubleDay, a division of Bantam Doubleday Dell Publishing Group, Inc., 1988).

2. Macrina Wiederkehr, O.S.B., *Seasons of Your Heart: Prayers and Reflections, Revised and Expanded* (New York, NY: HarperCollins Publishers, 1991).

3. Clarissa Pinkola Estes, Ph.D., *Women Who Run With the Wolves: Myths and Stories of the Wild Woman Archetype* (New York, NY: Ballantine Books, a division of Random House, Inc., 1992, 1995).

4. Katherine Mansfield, From *Winter Grief, Summer Grace* (Minneapolis, MN: Augsburg Fortress, 1995).

From Generation to Generation

5. *Daily Gazette,* Redwood Gazette Publishing Co., Inc. Volume 1, No. 98, August 11, 1932.

Mic's Message—Two Years Later

6. *Christopher News Note,* number 363, 12 East 48th St, New York, NY 10017.

7. Antoinette Bosco, *Coincidences: Touched by a Miracle* (Mystic, CT: Twenty-Third Publications, 1998).

Revelations of Love

8. Adolfo Quezada, *Catholic Vision,* Desert column, August, 2002.

Healing Resources from Resurrection Press

MOURNING SICKNESS
The Art of Grieving
Keith Smith

"Mourning Sickness . . . is a thought-provoking book about the art of living; its profound message has the power to change our lives. —**Geri Madak**

No. RP 184/04 ISBN 1-878718-85-1   **Price: $8.95**

HEALING YOUR GRIEF
Sr. Ruthann Williams, O.P.

"Sr. Ruthann . . . shares her insights as to what to say and be in the midst of death and what not to say and not to be." —**Msgr. Thomas Hartman**

No. RP 530/04 ISBN 1-878718-29-0   **Price: $7.95**

HEART PEACE
Embracing Life's Adversities
Adolfo Quezada

"This is one of the most authentic books I have ever read on the gut wrenching conditions that cause or lead to human suffering. . . . His book is a gift, allowing others to be the beneficiaries of his spiritual journey."
—**Antoinette Bosco**

No. RP 117/04 ISBN 1-878718-52-5   **Price: $9.95**

THE EDGE OF GREATNESS
Empowering Meditations for LIfe
Joni Woelfel

"Here is a woman whose courageous and passionate spirit has enabled her to step over the edge of greatness. She knows how to walk on water, because she has kept her eyes on the One who created the waters. Read this book and be blessed." —**Macrina Wiederkehr, OSB**

No. RP 134/04 ISBN 1-878718-93-2
Price: $9.95

www.catholicbookpublishing.com

Additional Titles Published by Resurrection Press, a Catholic Book Publishing Imprint

A Rachel Rosary *Larry Kupferman*	$4.50
A Season in the South *Marci Alborghetti*	$10.95
Blessings All Around *Dolores Leckey*	$8.95
Catholic Is Wonderful *Mitch Finley*	$4.95
Days of Intense Emotion *Keeler/Moses*	$12.95
Discernment *Chris Aridas*	$8.95
Feasts of Life *Jim Vlaun*	$12.95
From Holy Hour to Happy Hour *Francis X. Gaeta*	$7.95
Grace Notes *Lorraine Murray*	$9.95
Healing through the Mass *Robert DeGrandis, SSJ*	$9.95
Our Grounds for Hope *Fulton J. Sheen*	$7.95
Healing Your Grief *Ruthann Williams, OP*	$7.95
Heart Peace *Adolfo Quezada*	$9.95
How Shall We Pray? *James Gaffney*	$5.95
Lessons for Living from the 23rd Psalm *Victor Parachin*	$5.95
The Joy of Being an Altar Server *Joseph Champlin*	$5.95
The Joy of Being a Catechist *Gloria Durka*	$4.95
The Joy of Being a Eucharistic Minister *Mitch Finley*	$5.95
The Joy of Being a Lector *Mitch Finley*	$5.95
The Joy of Being an Usher *Gretchen Hailer, RSHM*	$5.95
The Joy of Marriage Preparation *McDonough/Marinelli*	$5.95
The Joy of Music Ministry *J.M. Talbot*	$6.95
The Joy of Praying the Rosary *James McNamara*	$5.95
The Joy of Preaching *Rod Damico*	$6.95
The Joy of Teaching *Joanmarie Smith*	$5.95
The Joy of Worshiping Together *Rod Damico*	$5.95
Lights in the Darkness *Ave Clark, O.P.*	$8.95
Loving Yourself for God's Sake *Adolfo Quezada*	$5.95
Magnetized by God *Robert E. Lauder*	$8.95
Meditations for Survivors of Suicide *Joni Woelfel*	$8.95
Mother Teresa *Eugene Palumbo, S.D.B.*	$5.95
Mourning Sickness *Keith Smith*	$8.95
Personally Speaking *Jim Lisante*	$8.95
Prayers from a Seasoned Heart *Joanne Decker*	$8.95
Praying the Lord's Prayer with Mary *Muto/vanKaam*	$8.95
5-Minute Miracles *Linda Schubert*	$4.95
Sabbath Moments *Adolfo Quezada*	$6.95
Season of New Beginnings *Mitch Finley*	$4.95
Season of Promises *Mitch Finley*	$4.95
Sometimes I Haven't Got a Prayer *Mary Sherry*	$8.95
St. Katharine Drexel *Daniel McSheffery*	$12.95
What He Did for Love *Francis X. Gaeta*	$5.95
Woman Soul *Pat Duffy, OP*	$7.95
You Are My Beloved *Mitch Finley*	$10.95

For a free catalog call 1-800-892-6657
www.catholicbookpublishing.com